MW00826993

JOURNEY PAST HUMAN LIMITATIONS

THROUGH A VISIONARY'S EYES . . .
MAKE YOUR WAY TO THE WONDERS
OF THE BLUE CRYSTAL PLANET

ETHEL E. CRITES

Jan-Carol
Publishing, Inc

"every story needs a book."

Journey Past Human Limitations
Through a Visionary's Eyes . . .
Make Your Way to the Wonders of the Blue Crystal Planet
Ethel E. Crites

Published August 2015
Express Editions
Imprint of Jan-Carol Publishing, Inc.
All rights reserved

ISBN: 978-1-939289-70-4
Library of Congress Control Number: 2015950718

You may contact the publisher:
Jan-Carol Publishing, Inc.
PO Box 701
Johnson City, TN 37605
publisher@jancarolpublishing.com
jancarolpublishing.com

This book is dedicated to my father, Rev. Gabriel Julius Fodor, who, in my early years, taught and inspired me to believe that all things are possible.

To my mother, Elizabeth Ann Fodor, who guided me intuitively through my dream state to come to the realization of my ability to connect with the Blue Crystal Planet.

To my daughter, Cherrie Crites Foster, who encouraged me to follow my spiritual path, and my passion for writing.

To my son, Robert Dale Crites, who gave me strength and the perseverance to pursue my mission in bringing this information to the world.

To my beloved husband, Bert Hobert Lincoln Crites, Jr., who has been my guiding spirit in presenting this material which awakens humanity to the knowledge of the existence of other worlds.

To Cosmos, my Bichon Frise dog, who was always Bert's buddy and was my wonderful, wonderful healing companion.

Special thanks to my graphic designer, Tara Sizemore, for bringing my front cover idea to life.

FOREWORD

Linda Aurora Foxx, Editor

It was a joy editing the amazing material from the channeled writing of Ethel Crites. The wealth of material was challenging, and yet flowed into an organized composition with the guidance of Darius, the primary master in spirit who, assisted in the writing. I always requested his presence before starting an editing session, and immediately sensed his close, loving countenance and wise assistance in providing just the right words when needed.

As editor, I found myself actually visiting the Blue Crystal beings triggered by Ethel's words as she described her experiences and discoveries as she was whirled into the environment of the cosmos and this high frequency world. Sometimes I would be shown a vibrant, living picture of what she was describing and the glorious beings that were patiently trying to describe their way of life so Ethel could convey this back to the Earth. Ethel was guided to put into written words the concepts of a planet culture without a language as we know it. It was most challenging to find expressions that portrayed the merriment, effortless ecstasy and delight that these beings exuded. Sometimes more information was required, and Darius would have Ethel again go into trance and bring back more detail for the clarity that was needed.

The material in the book contains a wealth of information about life in higher realms, angelic interaction and assistance for the Earth, and it is beyond words to describe what actually took place in Ethel's journeys. As she said repeatedly, ". . . there just isn't a language to accurately convey the love, beauty, peace, and higher thinking that is the paradigm in the cosmic dimensions beyond the Earth." This book is an opportunity for the reader to enter into a spiritual journey of multidimensional exploration with the Blue Crystal beings as their guide.

Linda Aurora Foxx, B.S., M.S., ordained minister with the Brigade of Light.,
Director of Aquarian Consciousness Fellowship, Asheville, NC

CONTENTS

INTRODUCTION

This labor of love has been in progress for over 20 years, commencing in 1988. It developed in a way that may be challenging for me to communicate to you due to the nature of the channeling and the need for an appropriate order for the information. To fully understand the esoteric meaning of this book, being acquainted with channeled writing, otherwise known as automatic writing, would be helpful. For the novice to this method of communication, I define channeled writing as an individual allowing his Higher Self, mind and heart to be used for information to intuitively come through his physical body in a form that can be spoken or written. Another description is allowing your soul and mind to know no boundaries, and to tap into the outer sources to the eternal heavens. This is done lovingly in accordance with the soul contract and will of the person doing the channeling. Writers, artists, musicians, and other creative people do this all the time, but not all recognize what they do or how they are able to achieve such feats and accomplishments. The spiritual and moral purity of the channel determines the accuracy and clarity of the information. It is my humble prayer that only truth may manifest in my words as I bring this information in to the Earth plane.

One way to tune into a channel frequency is to "Level Up" or turning on your conscious mind and to think in the light or visualize a light bulb in your head and all around you which would raise you into a higher frequency. The beings doing the channeling from the other side or higher dimensions have to learn how to lower their frequency or "anchor down." They tell me to always keep the dials open, so we can retune and refine our instruments together, and they say they are always ready to give assistance or receive our requests. It is actually the nature of our soul to open up our minds, hearts, and souls to channeling, and in the future, it will be as natural as talking on the telephone.

When doing channeled writing, one has little control over the product. The information is given to a person when in the alpha state of meditation, and it is in no particular order. I always prepare by surrounding myself with protective white and violet light and stating that only information which can come through the white light of Christ consciousness is welcome. I choose to relinquish control over the time when the information comes through. It comes at any time of the day or night. I would wake up at 2:00 a.m., write for an hour and go back to sleep without any difficulty. I put down each section as a separate chapter, and only now am attempting to put these in a reader-friendly format.

The first time this channeled material was conveyed through me, I was in a meditative state and my guides came through and began to discuss with me telepathically that there were many kinds of expressions of creation or species in different worlds in a myriad of infinite universes. I was somewhat aware of this, since I travel to other dimensions and planets almost every night in my sleep, as most of us do.

They explained that humanity on Earth usually considered itself as the only life form in the universe. Only recently some scientists and philosophers have hypothesized that there is the possibility of life existing in our and other universes, possibly even not carbon based. The guides told me I would soon be visiting and learning about our sister planet, the Blue Crystal Planet. Most of the material was given to me by an entity who called himself Darius from the Third Galaxy. I, in a trance state, was guided and instructed to prepare my physical body in such a way that my ethereal or light body could free itself and be able to be guided and tuned into the various planes and dimensions to be taught universal knowledge about other worlds, planets and beings in the heavenly realms. Thus, I was taken further along in my journey of love and unending curiosity about these other worlds in this magnificent cosmos.

When I silently questioned the guides as to how I would explain this channeling to the questioning person, they urged me to refer to the Bible where the Master Christ taught in John 14:2, "In my Father's house are many mansions. If it were not so, I would have told you." The mansions I was shown were not of the third dimension, yet they were places teeming with indescribable beauty and life in higher frequencies, far beyond the Earth concept of physical mansions.

I found myself being inspired in different ways and on many levels. Sometimes, while in this altered state, I felt as though I was writing three books at a time. For this reason there has sometimes been a sense of disconnection. I believe this is a process of writing in free form and bringing up material on different levels of consciousness. In actuality, it was imparted to me by the beings that this is the way our brain processes thought on an unconscious level, and we lose much when we try to bring up the material to a conscious level and "make sense of it." The free-flow is richer, and I hope you will permit yourself to be exposed to this and enjoy it without necessarily looking for logic. Logical thinking is mechanical, computer-like thinking. I believe that free-flow thinking, emotions and automatic writing are on a higher level of expression and are what makes humans superior to machines. I hope you feel free to allow yourself to explore this process and find a new joy in it.

It is my hope that regardless of one's previous spiritual or religious experiences or level of interest, every reader will find something in this book that speaks to them, whether it is simply fun, a deeper understanding of the universe, or any level in between. In the past I read books in my adolescence, re-read them in my twenties and then re-read them in my forties. Each time, I found some new delightful insight that I had missed the previous time. It had nothing to do with the book itself, because the writer did not re-write it, but rather the fact that I was at a different stage of evolving in my life and had new perceptions and perspectives. One may want, after finishing this book, to reread some of their old favorites and see whether they can find new levels of meaning in them as well. Best wishes to you, and may the magnificent energy of the Blue Crystal Planet merge with you, so that you may be further inspired and uplifted in your evolution!

CHAPTER ONE

An Introduction from Darius

"The Earth is not aligned with the rest of the planets in your solar system, and in order to become aligned, you must become more aware of the light within your souls."

It was May 15, 1988, 6:30 a.m., and I awakened with a dream of being far, far away from the Earth. I felt an urgency to write. Although I was well versed in channeled writing coming through me, it was my first contact with a magnificent life form from a place I had never visited called the Blue Crystal Planet. I clairvoyantly saw through my third eye a group of extremely radiant, ethereal humanoid beings, nearly transparent, slowly approach our bed and telepathically ask if they could communicate. I nodded permission and they asked me to go to my computer, so I almost sleep-walked to my desk and prepared to type as I listened within. Thus, began a discourse that was to forever change my life.

A being of immense brightness stepped forward. I had never seen such light and luminescence, and I was overcome with the great love and presence he portrayed and emanated. He was a tall, handsome male being clothed in rainbow hues and other unearthly colors of light. The room was filled with a fragrant, flower-like aroma that resembled gardenias. I felt intensely loved, cherished and almost overcome with the energy that surrounded me.

He said, "I am Darius, the ruler of the Third Universe. We are from a parallel paradigm of a higher frequency and more evolved than the Earth and are a sister planet to you named the Blue Crystal Planet. Our planet and its inhabitants, the crystal beings, were brought in alignment with your Earth in order to assist and influence its many changes leading up to and beyond 2012. The Earth is not aligned with the rest of the planets in your solar system, and in order to become aligned, you must become more aware of the light within your souls. The sun was devised from many material particles of the other planets to give this planet light for existence. So, the Earth is literally borrowing the light. The Blue Crystal Planet is in a higher dimensional frequency and does not need sunlight to exist, due to the species of light bodies that have developed their own light. They have more of the DNA molecular structure of which humankind will soon discover. The Blue Crystal beings are quite evolved and live in a peaceful existence. They can move their bodies by floating, because they can defy your gravitational pull."

"I have been observing your clairvoyant and precise channeling talents and your sincere eagerness to help others. I am asking your permission to work with you to bring forth information that may assist humans. It is vital that the people of the Earth have the opportunity to learn and absorb this instruction."

I was told that humankind occasionally is able to catch a glimpse of these beings that live in this parallel existence. People may sense them as angels who help with some daily events, but also, they assist humankind in evolving through inspiring ideas or opportune circumstances. They protect and guide us in both the sleeping and awake state.

The urgency of his voice caught my attention, and my heart began to pound. I recognized the Christ-like energy he radiated, and I felt honored by his request. My fingers raced over the keyboard and I began to shiver, and I pulled my robe around my shoulders as I began to type.

Darius went on to explain, "The paradigm shift for the Earth as it evolves into the fourth and fifth dimensions is slowly occurring and will be even more rapidly speeding up as that which is known as time, diminishes. This calls for quick and effective resources to meet the needs of a desperate and searching humanity. One of our major concerns is to see that the human race evolves peacefully without destroying itself and the planet. It will take many Earth years for humanity to develop a higher frequency and achieve what will be called the splendid and pristine 'New Earth.' Humans will eventually learn to use their universal mind, not the social mind that they now use. They have been programmed by the many humans that surround them to take in more from their dense minds than from the inner spiritual, electrical, and magnetic energies that make up their vastness. Humans are unaware that they are a universe within themselves and that when the Great Master, the Christ, stated that 'The Kingdom of God is within you,' that is what He meant! Humanity has the ability to heal themselves and their entire population if they would reprogram their minds and hearts that they have the power to do so."

Immense curiosity engulfed me as I pondered what he was saying. I could only wonder what extraordinary experiences might lay before me. My heart was so overcome with gratitude that I had been chosen and contacted by such a powerful being. The sense of presence he exuded was almost more than I could take in and comprehend, yet it had happened to me; it was more than a passing dream. I simply had to believe it. The rippling of words on my computer was object proof. I had an idea that soon I would actually be a traveler to the Blue Crystal Planet.

Of course, I was well aware of the dramatic and rapid changes taking place on the Earth. Anyone who was even half awake felt and sensed immense upheaval and turmoil both within and without in their everyday life. This chaos is due to the beginning of massive spiritual, political, social, and physical upheavals associated with the year 2012. Through the ages there have always been some humans who studied metaphysics and knew the truth about the planets, ascended masters, and constant evolution of the universes. More humans are now aware that every 26,500 years the galaxy passes through the photon energy belt and moves forward in a giant step of evolution. That step was initiated on the date of December 21, 2012. Although it is chaotic, it is also a time of great personal and societal growth and joy as we recreate a New Earth and return to a peaceful civilization.

I knew that benevolent extraterrestrials and multitudes of angelic beings were drawing closer to us in recent years in order to assist humankind in this undertaking. I believed the nature of their contact was always kind, quietly urging us forward with suggestions and ideas for reinventing our paradigm. Some are present in our major institutions looking like everyday humans, but persistently supporting and demonstrating an agenda that replaces greed and violence with love and harmony.

Previously, I had brief encounters with E.T.'s in meditation and out in nature, but Darius was making a direct request for me to work with them to assist the Earth. I felt unequal to the task, but I was reminded that I was well known for accuracy in the intuitive work I did with the public. So, I made the decision to move forward with Darius and stated that I would accept his request. At that point I was gently led back to my bed and fell into a deep, satisfying sleep, and awoke only half believing what had occurred. Only by going to my computer and reading the words Darius had spoken, did I allow myself to fully believe that it had really happened.

The next few days I let memories of Darius fade in and out of my consciousness as I went about my life working with my counseling clients, doing the everyday housewife chores, the usual social events, and, of course, being with my beloved husband, Bert, who was an amazing person. He told me when I first met him that he was different, from a faraway place, and that he had brought his special talents and energies to assist in the healing of the planet.

However, for a few days, I did not mention the contact from Darius, just wanting to savor the high frequency of his contact that recent night. It made me ponder even more just where I was from and who I was, because in meditation and dreams I often left my body and found myself in many crystalline cities of light that seemed familiar. Or, I would sail the celestial highways that led to planets similar to the Earth and attend classes led by the ascended masters. It is my belief that we all are doing these things, but we don't remember because the veil of forgetfulness that most of us are cloaked with at birth has not yet been removed.

A few evenings later, I encountered Bert peacefully resting in his study. "There's something I want to tell you, darling," I hesitantly whispered.

He looked up, a little surprised that I was whispering. I felt like a school girl confessing a wondrous happening. My heart was pounding, and I felt extremely uplifting frequencies engulfing my body. I wanted so much to share this with my soulmate.

"Well, you know how you and I have discussed our experiences with beings from other dimensions and how mysterious it is and yet so extremely unearthly and wonderful . . . well, something new happened to me, and I am so excited!" The words came pouring out of me as I related my encounter with Darius and my decision to work with him.

He beckoned me to sit beside him on the couch and placed his arm around my shoulders. As always, I welcomed his warm acceptance of me and my intuitive abilities, and he was his usual reassuring and encouraging self. "Well, why not? You go to other planets in your ethereal body almost every night in your sleep. I think this is an amazing opportunity to help. Why wouldn't you be asked? Why wouldn't you be chosen to bring this information out to the public?" he countered. "I think, by all means, you should do it!"

I relaxed into the cozy warmth of his love and acceptance of me, and I, again, marveled at the depth of our relationship and understanding of each other. We had been together in many previous lives, and this lifetime was designed to further unite us and move us forward in experiences of oneness and service. I sighed in relaxed happiness, and wondered when my next meeting with Darius would occur. At this point, I hoped it would be quite soon.

Two nights later instruction began. I was awakened and went to my computer. Again, the luminous presence of Darius accompanied by other beings approached me. After loving greetings, he invited me to receive information that would prepare me to go into the atmosphere of the Blue Crystal Planet while I was continuing to type the information on Earth. I was surprised and excited that I would be actually going to another planet in a conscious state, but I did not understand how my physical body could continue typing in my office.

I moved rapidly as the information poured forth on my computer from Darius. "When you first enter the atmosphere of the Blue Crystal Planet, you are already in your ethereal or light body, so that you can literally float about and see, feel and sense the existence of other beings there. You feel as though you are riding on a cloud and are quite light. It is as if you have taken off your outer clothing, or physical embodiment, which is cumbersome and would not adjust easily to our wondrous magnetic environment. It is a sensation analogous to being in a dream state while in the physical body and moving easily in the light and your mind only. In this environment one moves in the ethereal body and the cosmic mind. You will need to start preparing your physical body and mind to be able to continuously channel this information while in a trance-like state. To do this you will learn to relax your mind and body and to surrender to your higher conscious being or Higher Self. This, of course, will be acquired over time and practice with our guidance as you meditate."

Thus, ended a brief session with Darius. I reflected on the part about continuously channeling this information while in a trance-like state. To me this meant my physical body would continue typing at my computer while a non-physical part of me would be experiencing spiritual awareness on another planet millions of miles away. This was truly mind boggling and stretched my comprehension of what the human being was capable of doing. It brought to mind information that had been related to me recently that all parts of the universe are contained in each cell of our body. It is merely by changing our thoughts and conditioning that we unleash limitless possibilities of what the soul can achieve, where its consciousness can travel, and what information it can return with and pass on to others.

CHAPTER TWO

My First Visit to the Blue Crystal Planet

"ALL SOULS MEET IN THEIR DIVINE LIGHT!"

Over the next several days, I spent much time in deep meditation asking that I be prepared and begin to acquire the additional spiritual skills I would need for the channeling work. I felt the presence of many guides and masters working with me on higher levels. I was told that I would learn more about these skills as I actually began to use them in traveling to the Blue Crystal Planet.

One day, as I sat quietly at my computer in meditation and after my usual protective prayers, I asked Darius to be present as I offered time for the work at hand. Immediately, he and several Blue Crystal guides appeared. I found myself slipping away from my third-dimensional conscious state. I felt my physical body getting lighter and lighter, almost the weight of a feather. I was, then, suddenly zoomed up away from the ground. I began looking back at my beautiful planet Earth getting smaller and smaller out in the enormous space. I glanced around at the multitude of various stars and caught glimpses of planets spinning and spinning, like tops in their rotation courses. At that moment I felt a spiraling motion and found myself also swirling in space, similar to the planets. However, I did not feel motion with my body as one does on the Earth's surface. Rather, I was floating like a cloud. I looked at my ethereal body and could actually see through myself, and I appeared to consist of iridescent colors. It was all truly fascinating to me.

At that point, I felt the presence of many angelic-like beings, as well as the beings from the Blue Crystal Planet, navigating me through the process of traveling through space. I was told not to fear, since the guides were with me and would not allow anything to happen. I felt an enormous amount of love and protection from these beings, as well as immense, indescribable anticipation and excitement. I experienced a relaxed and safe feeling and was enjoying the journey immensely.

When I arrived in their super magnetic energy field, I felt like I was spinning, yet moving at a very fast speed. They began to tell me more about what to expect on this journey. They communicated telepathically rather than verbally. It was so easy to converse with them that I found myself wondering why we did not have conversations on Earth in the same manner. As my ethereal body was floating out in space, I experienced being as free as a bird in flight. Yet, amazingly enough, there was still a part of me sitting at my computer.

Intuitively, without being told, I started sensing that we were fast approaching the Blue Crystal Planet as it was coming toward me and appeared to be revolving, although it was standing still. The wonder and beauty of the planet is difficult to describe, as it was breathtaking, shining in colors I had never seen before. It was so magnificent and bright that I could hardly take it all in. The planet was surrounded by the most beautiful and brilliant blue colored crystals of a shade and saturation I had never seen on Earth. It was difficult for me to focus, as every area demanded my attention. I felt unbelievably happy and joyful.

As we came closer and closer, I became somewhat apprehensive due to the newness of this experience. There was an energy emitted from the planet that overcame my hesitation, and I sensed it was loving, soothing and peaceful. I felt captivated and overwhelmed, yet comfortable, as though I were finally coming home.

The guides somehow started working with my ethereal body balancing the energy and frequency of the vibrations I encountered, so that my entry into the atmosphere of the planet would be comfortable. They appeared to want to avoid my experiencing a sense of shock and disconnection. I could actually sense the energy change in my light body. At that moment I was enveloped in a warm vibration of love and peace; I knew that I had entered one of the heavenly realms.

As I was floating about and observing in my light body, I seemed to have a new type of vision. I had the ability to see all things with my entire body, including my changed molecular and cellular structure. It was as if I could see everything at once and not just one thing at a time such as a tree or group of trees. This is difficult to describe, yet, I had a wonderful feeling of taking in the whole picture at once. The beings kept adjusting my energy frequency and modifying my state with its new surroundings. It was like our astronauts traveling in the outer space with their specially designed gear made to protect them. I, too, needed to be protected at all times.

First, as I entered the planet's atmosphere, I began to see misty forms, as if in a fog. Then, I saw magnificent crystal buildings. Their blue hue was like none I could have imagined and had a sparkling aura like diamonds. The buildings were pyramid-shaped and sometimes dome shaped. They were fully lighted with the energy of crystal power. They looked like the many facets of a brilliant jewel or crystal, and I was able to move through them by changing the frequency of my vibration, which I accomplished with the help of my guides. I was told that each building was coded and protected from any possible outside harm.

The guides told me that the Blue Crystal Planet does not need sunlight or electric light as Earth needs, since these species have bodies that have developed their own light. They have more activation of their DNA molecular structure, which will be discovered soon in humankind.

Their light bodies are more evolved and have a peaceful energy. They are able to move by floating, for they defy the gravitational pull. There is no night, only lighted days. In the cosmos, there is darkness, so the light of the planet is like a beacon in the sky or universe. My guides informed me that these beings are here not only to assist us, but also to have the experience of living in and learning about the material worlds of Earth and other planets with which they interact.

One of the beings explained to me that I would get glimpses of many different forms of the light beings. They differed not only from the human physical bodies, but also from human ethereal bodies, for they did not mirror exactly our humanoid shape. I was warned that although their form may resemble human form, it was important that I remember that they were not human and, therefore, I could not think of them in such terms. They can actually take on many different shapes, which they can create at a moment's notice.

When I arrived at the outer part of the planet, their tour guides took me to a special station where I was given more orientation and instructions on how to maneuver. They somehow adjusted my frequencies and fine-tuned my ethereal body so that I would not become confused or disoriented, and they were lovingly protective of me. They gave me an analogy so I would better understand the process. It would be like putting on scuba diving gear for the ocean, but instead it was a spiritual "consciousness gear" that allowed me to move on their planet. So, as we make adjustments to move about on our planet Earth whether it is the ocean or an airplane in the sky, or a missile in space, I, too, needed to make necessary adjustments to be able to transport myself on their planet and in their environment.

I was told that each group of beings inhabiting a particular place on their planet has its own genetic code, within which they could transform their appearance. They told me, however, that for my personal tour they would make adjustments so that I could envision them closer to my own light body. Since they have both a greater quantity and a deeper spectrum of lights and sounds, I was not prepared for the many colors I had never seen and sound tones I had never heard. They chose blue, pink, green, violet, purple, white, yellow, and gold, because I was familiar with these, in order to help me feel more at home. The tones sent rivulets of delight through my light body and were truly heavenly frequencies. They adjusted the frequencies of the waves of the colors in order to enable my ethereal sight to tolerate them easily. There was the danger that I might not be able to adjust and could be so disturbed by what I saw and heard that I would be propelled back to my physical body in the Earth's environment. The effect of this would make me wonder what happened to me, as though I had awakened from a deep sleep and dream. The beings were determined not to let this happen, for they wanted me to have the experiences they had planned and take the memories back to Earth. They asked me whether I understood what they were doing and what was happening, and I nodded.

They went on to explain that we humans must process by thinking out an issue and then communicating it through verbal sound that will resonate with the other person. I was told that on the Blue Crystal Planet communication was different from what I was used to on Earth. For example, greetings occurred by a type of integration or infusion, by the blending of energies. The blending caused one to feel the other's energy throughout the entire being's mind, body and soul level, whereas, on Earth, we often merely hug and maybe kiss to greet. Their integration of energies is also used to send and receive messages about their work .

It may also be about what they were thinking, cleansing, healing or readjusting in their life at that particular moment. They could read each other's messages instantly, respond to their need or desires, or maybe just give affirmation or validation. Love, healing and communication all occurred telepathically. They also had the ability to do a complete readout of the other being instantaneously. Their lips did not move and there were no sounds. Instead, I saw sound waves emitted and information transmitted. I heard with my inner being, rather than with my ears. The frequencies varied and the various colors matched up with the sound intonations. I could not help but marvel at what a beautiful sight and a remarkable thing that was.

The guides and light beings accompanying me told me that the light from the buildings was so bright that one could not see it with the naked human eye. For this reason, they accompanied me every step of the way. It was their way of protecting me. I was told that this protection expressed itself by the transformation of my physical body to a light body before I arrived, which resulted in the buildings appearing like a mirrored reflections. Once I adjusted, I would literally float through the crystal forms of these structures. I was warned that I would feel a burst of energy and feel so exhilarated that I would want to stay in this mode forever. However, in order to move on, I would need help in being transported. Without the beings' help, I might be stuck in one mode and not continue my journey.

I was told that as I continued to move, I would come upon certain things that I would be unable to recognize since there is no comparison to them on Earth. There would be unusual types of machines and much more advanced computer systems. Although I could recognize sounds and distinguish various lights and colors, I could not do this with my naked physical ears and eyes. These sounds of love and harmony came into the light body and filled it. I felt a tingling or pulsations within my light body that I had never experienced before. They told me that should I have a physical disease or ailment, I would be healed instantly. This healing came through the ethereal body first, and afterward, it was translated and recorded in the physical body. To understand it easily, it was explained to me that this process is similar to updating software on a computer. To become disease-free is a form of reprogramming. I understood that when these regenerative energies happened to me, I would return to Earth as a revived person.

I told Darius that I was curious about their community structures, so I was zoomed up toward something we would call a "city" and they called a gathering place. They explained that all their structures were made of crystal or diamond-like material, for these elements are far advanced from the nature elements on Earth. He explained that there would be gathering places set up with iridescent color, but of crystal formation. Then, I might come across places where there may be a dominant color or frequency like green, blue, violet, red, tan, or more neutral.

Their cities or places of congregation were determined by the various purposes or work of the light beings that inhabited them. They have shops, malls or large buildings and streets or recreational places, such as parks on Earth, but their color and frequency determine the type of place or dwelling. One could see through the buildings with spiral structures. Every building spiraled either up or down or sideways unlike any configuration with which I was familiar. I stopped and paused while suspended, taking in the overview of these unusual spiral arrangements. They were not actually in different colors, but in a variety of hues. As I passed over them, I heard different sounds and tones coming from each one. They were not placed in a row, but were often overlapping without actually touching or impinging on each other's space. Some of the buildings were fairly simple, and some were actually constructed with many winding features.

It appeared that these cities were dwelling places for masters that focused on a particular area. They each appeared to have a theme. These masters were not only working on projects on the Blue Crystal Planet, but also for various other planets. They were also connected to other dimensions and were able to multi-task within their area of responsibility and expertise. Some were actually able to work simultaneously in more than one area.

All at once, I was instantly attracted to a vast array of lights below me that appeared as an array of blazing purple or violet color. When the guide followed my gaze, he explained, "This area is what we call the Holiest of the Holy or the Violet City, and it is where beings similar to priests or ministers reside. They are the wise ones who create and recreate the many texts or Bibles that have been given to human-kind. They keep updating the information, as humans evolve to better understandings and interpretations of God or the God Source."

Sensing my curiosity and interest, the guides sort of swirled me into this place of immeasurable joy and intense illumination with chambers or divisions of operation as on Earth. I was shown levels like our colleges which had levels of freshmen, sophomores, juniors, seniors, and graduates. There did not seem to be endings or completions to each level here, and each was continued into infinity. They told me it was because there is no end here, just change, movement and evolving. So, as I was entering these levels, I only felt the energy change and different coloration and frequencies. It was awesome!

There was a type of literal interpretation on a manuscript which was likened to our Bible. They said this is the level the Earth is on presently; however, I could sense or feel the next level where they were bringing about information through an event that is eventually forthcoming, similar to what we would call arrival of the Second Messiah. They were given this information to write about and interpret for us from God and His many teachers.

There are many master teachers, they told me, and they are bringing in the New Dawn. In the New Millennium we will have what we call New Age teachings, for this is the closest we can come at this time in developing our spirituality. It is through Divine Intervention that we begin to connect to our soul levels and to retrieve our forgotten teachings from the soul seed or that which has become disconnected. The way we can reconnect is through these Universal teachings and these divine beings are trained to do this by divine order. These are the master teachers, and some have incarnated in the Earth at times and others have not. These beings give off a violet and purple hue and are extremely bright, surrounded with brilliant, white light that fills their aura. They also have a type of halo above their heads indicating their connection to the God Source where all information is given or received. These beings, I would say, are not of the Earth, literally, for they are extremely advanced. They are revered and honored by all and among themselves. There is a type of hierarchy in the group, but not in our sense, and there is no jealousy or envy amongst them.

When I moved to the second level, I stood in reverence at what I was observing. I felt it was a great honor for me to even be there. They were interpreting the New Age wisdom, which, of course, was ancient wisdom, and they were receiving manifestations from higher levels which flowed in waves through their halos and into their being. They, then, translated this information given in waves such as it is given into our brains as thoughts, and somehow manipulated and transferred these into a type of machine, but it did not feel mechanical to me. When they had acquired a certain amount of information, they gathered into a circle and did a kind of ceremony. I heard a type of spherical music from another dimension, and they told me it was of the utmost or highest sound or intonation. Then, they came together and their colors swirled and merged into one hue which they said was the Oneness of All. Next, I saw a type of golden staff or rod that was manifested in vivid color swirl through the beings and connect their souls into one enormous soul. I had not seen anything like this!

They told me that our churches and religious ceremonies attempt to replicate this on primitive level, but they, too, teach us to honor the gods and to pay a type of homage. They, also, have this practice on their planet and come to the masses of their kind to offer their renderings or teachings. However, because these are master teachers they can actually have access to the divine that can join their soul into one mass soul. This is where they do their best work, because out of this mass comes the teachings in the light that is given to all and filters down to humankind.

ALL TEACHINGS OF THE DIVINE LEAD TO ONENESS! This is the most important lesson. They told me that when humankind can respect all religions, and the souls of all beings, then there will be heaven on Earth. We have a long way to go. They were working diligently to bring this information to us, and they told me that our mindset and soul set will merge and we will have the universal teachings within us. There will come a time when we do not need religion as we do today, for we will be able to dialogue and receive from the God Source direct.

Then, at my request, they explained more about the various levels in this most sacred city. The guide explained, "Humans can't achieve these levels because they must first master their souls before they can move forward, and then they will be in the frequency that was originally intended for them. The reason there are so-called levels is because of the various light frequencies. Should humans attempt to receive on higher levels, their bodies could not withstand the energies which is why these masters can withstand the finer frequencies and bring them down to the Earth's planetary level.

"The higher levels include more information about the various heavenly spheres and higher beings, but is difficult for humankind to learn in their present form due to the need for more development of their minds and brains. However, soon humans will learn about the higher heavens where ALL SOULS MEET IN THEIR DIVINE LIGHT!"

Now, as I was leaving this Violet City, I looked back to take in an overview of all its amazing beauty one more time. The crystallized buildings with all its diverse levels looked at first divided and separate, but as I continued to gaze, they merged into one blazing, magnificent purple form of the highest vibration that beckoned me to coalesce with them. In time, the guide said, "ALL WILL BE ONE."

Suddenly, I became aware that I was typing at my computer. Much Earth time had passed; the clock said several hours. With a quiet, peaceful floating, I had returned to Earth consciousness. I experienced an unbelievable and extremely enlightening journey. Darius told me it was a trial run to start to accustom me to the energy changes and that I succeeded in adapting quite well. It was with great regret that I left the high frequency of the Blue Crystal Planet, for now I was a part of it in a conscious state and I would never be the same. I sat in a daze at my computer reliving and recapturing the events of the day.

The next day, I ecstatically told Bert about my first encounter. At first, he was amazed that I could recall my experience so vividly.

"Actually, I should not be surprised, since you often remember glimpses of material that comes to you when you do intuitive channeling for clients," he remarked. "And this time you are being instructed to actually bring the information back for others to read and you are typing it."

I nodded, trying to assimilate all that I remembered.

"You know," I enthusiastically remarked, "there is an amazing difference in the frequency of the Blue Crystal Planet and here on Earth. It is like being in a heavenly realm rather than here on Earth with its many challenges and its limited paradigm. I see now the scintillating beauty of the higher dimensions even more clearly and there is a place in my heart that wasn't there before that visit. It does give me a glimpse of what the Earth will be like when it changes to the fourth and fifth dimensions."

CHAPTER THREE

The Nature of the Beings from the Blue Crystal Planet

"So, the reasons why you have some atmospheric changes in the weather
is because the many light beings, angels and guides as well as masters
and avatars are combining their efforts and their miraculous workings
to change the energy grid of the earth."

It was a cool fall Wednesday; however, there was a lot of warm energy exerting the power of light in my office as I was greeted by Darius. He stated that he wanted to offer more background information on the beings from his planet so humans would begin to understand what they were like. I was, once more, trance typing at the computer as he explained how the Blue Crystal Beings differ in body, mind and spirit from humans:

"We are in control of our planet and its environment and have complete freedom to expand on all levels, whereas, humans have been stuck in the same mind set and the same programs for eons of time. You see, the beings on our planet have a bird's eye view of your Earth. To us, you look like busy, busy ants building your homes with your heads stuck in the ground. However, when we look into your souls, we see another true being that is trying to find its way. That's why we have the patience to assist you and encourage your minds to higher levels of thinking and being.

"You are such busy people but sometimes busy with the wrong agenda. It is good to have order among the chaos, but to do repeated tasks over and over is futile in the growth of your soul. An example of this would be when you celebrate your holidays each and every year. The honor and significance is important, but the emphasis is totally wrong. Take the Christmas holiday. It is right to remember your Master Christ and his birthday; however, when the commercialism takes over, what is your priority and what does it teach your children and adults? It becomes a holiday of business and profit rather than just emphasizing the truth of the event. Other holidays are the same, such as Easter with an emphasis on the Bunny Rabbit and not on the soul-body resurrection of the master and avatar, the Christ. Each year is the same, rotating around the calendar of holidays. Why is this so?

"Would it not be more constructive to have new projects and holidays or celebrations honoring all cultures and races around the planet? Where is your creativity and your ability to step out of the box and begin to recreate your world with a better understanding of all humankind, and to become aware of your true selves and purpose? Humans talk about Peace on Earth, especially during the holiday season, yet they do not quite understand how to accomplish what it is they desire. If they continue hatred and wars, they will regress in their progress and desire to bring about peace. Peace cannot be brought about with anger, hatred, and killing. This is a barbaric viewpoint.

"It is necessary to communicate and understand all the various vibrations that are present in other governments and cultures. Each nation must be examined to see how they really operate in the way they govern their people, in the way they believe, in the way they look at other nations, in how they live, and how they desire to live. It is wrong to think that one is better than the other. Each operates on its own frequency and must take time to elevate or progress to the next. You cannot make another country think like yours any more than they can make yours think differently.

"It is time to put arms and weapons down and to back away and let each nation govern itself in the way that works for it. Once humankind removes their weapons, there will be more time to negotiate and facilitate the desire to assist each other in positive ways. The most important thing to learn is to love their neighbor as thyself! Is this not what the Master Christ came to teach?

"This concept will take time, but the brothers on the Blue Crystal Planet are coming in droves to help teach and work with these negative energies to bring about more peace. They have the ability to read out all the energy grids of all places on the Earth. They work with the energy balance and put into place a new grid that will filter down into the Earth's atmosphere and also placing in motion frequencies that will work together, unlike the shockwaves and static that have been occurring. So, the reason you have some atmospheric changes in the weather is because the many light beings, angels, and guides as well as masters and avatars are combining their efforts and their miraculous workings to change the energy grid of the Earth.

"There will be many movements and some, yes, destructive, waves in order to smooth out the lines and connections and to reconstruct the right frequencies to bring about a level of calmness and resistance to destroy. This will happen in your lifetime. There will always be dissension on the Earth, but there will and can be the desire to have peace and understanding.

"Once humans understand these differences in the way others think and their belief systems, they can begin to bring the anomalies together in light oscillations, so as to filter out the static and frequencies that harm or bring about shockwaves. They must learn to do this on a quantum physics level, as well as in the way they think and believe. Only in this way will they begin to bring more harmony and peace.

"Continuing with the discussion of the material emphasis of holidays on the Earth, the beings on our planet surround themselves with much flexibility and creativity. We are not dependent upon currency like your dollar, but rather on the love and well-being of the planet as a whole. Yes, there are teams and committees to come up with ideas and new blueprints that are always in flux and change. This keeps the light bodies active in their own creativity and able to share these new ideas and changes without the bureaucracy that is so prevalent in your world. It is not necessary to operate on a monetary system that could break down at any time. Just look at your stock markets and how they operate. On your sister planet we have the means to take care of each soul and are, therefore, not limited by the same constraints. You all go by a special way of organizing your world and you have programed yourselves to believe that is the only way to live and exist.

"What would happen if you chose to change your programming gradually? For instance, place your emphasis on hunger on your planet. Each continent could devise ingenious and improved methods to feed its own people and share their own creative ideas with others and, as a result, literally wipe out hunger. The agriculturists could teach young people to grow their own organic gardens in the country and cities using all the empty spaces such as abandoned lots or roof tops. If each American chose to donate a dollar and used that money, these skills could be accomplished in a short time. When your people nourish their bodies, they also nourish their souls by each one contributing to the well-being of the entire planet.

"These are just examples of how each one of you could promote faster evolution among your people. You would have to place the implementation of these projects in the hands of trusted people. Your government is not ready to do this, due to the many greedy souls that are governing your Earth. These tasks must be led by your churches and spiritual groups that truly have the right mindset and the desire to serve humankind. By taking the many tours on the Blue Crystal Planet, other planets, and dimensions, you will see the vast differences in evolution and begin to really understand how Earthlings have been stuck in the same mindset and program."

Darius paused to allow me to digest what he was saying, as I was somewhat startled by his enlightened understanding of the condition of the Earth. He was totally in tune with my reality as a counselor working with people struggling to move forward in their lives and attempting to get out of the "box." I wondered what the next steps would be for us to evolve more rapidly.

Darius, observing my thoughts continued: "We will give more information about how you can better accomplish the task before you and even how beings from other planets that are more advanced can assist in the process. Some of these new ideas will be foreign such as how to create new materials and manifest cutting-edge ideas to make the major changes. There is a type of programming your brains require in order to accept change and to begin to modify your current paradigm. You must have faith and not allow other influences in or negativity to enter your minds. You can do this by allowing cosmic thinking to replace social thinking and, as a result, it will become much easier to change the disk of your program."

Hearing him speak, I felt sort of mind boggled over the immensity of the task that lay before us, yet there was so many reasons for hope. For a minute, I felt myself just look down on the Earth with all her many problems and challenges, but I also felt relief that we were being assisted by so many beings of higher frequency. I sat back and sighed.

Sensing that I was more relaxed, Darius sent a breathtaking ray of violet and gold energy around my body as I gave my attention to the computer, and my whole being was refreshed and readjusted to the task at hand.

"So, continuing with how we are different from you, as fourth-dimensional beings, we are in light-illuminated bodies. This is the reason we look like crystals or specks of light or stars to humans when you catch a glimpse of us."

I asked, "Why do you call yourselves Blue Crystal beings?"

He answered, "Because we usually appear blue to you due to the influence of your blue Earth planet. Out in space, the Earth appears blue because of the many oceans and lakes. So, the sun that governs the light and warmth of this planet reflects this color to us. Actually, to each other and sometimes to you, we do not appear as one color. We are in a spectrum of light that diffuses many or multi-colors depending upon our level of experience on our planet, as well as on other planets and galaxies.

"You may ask, 'What is it like to be a type of a light-transparent form?' We would ask you, 'What is it like to be a physical form or one that is flesh and blood?' That is a difficult concept for us for we would have to go to the so-called Akashic Records to look up our DNA code to help remember when we experienced a physical body on your planet Earth. We could then place the coded information in a type of scanner that would bring up that lifetime or lifetimes on a visual screen which would give us a remembrance of what it was like. Now, you, too, have a remembrance of your heavenly home or the origin from where you came, but it is much more difficult for you to access because you are stuck in a conscious mode and a belief system that keeps you trapped for the moment, if you know what I mean. It is now coming to the forefront that humanity can access this information for yourselves if you wish to expand your conscious level.

"In order to do this, you only need to know that your reality is of a temporary nature and that this cosmic reality is your true one. So, with your physical senses you are limited, however, with your sixth, seventh, and eighth senses which are part of the cosmic mind, you are unlimited and eternal. Humans can use their soul seed within each of them to learn more about the higher self that they truly are and not the illusionary one that they believe they are. It is of limiting value to be stuck in the physical mode, and of infinite value to be free and allow your souls to soar, develop and grow by leaps and bounds."

"We have the ability to diffuse light or to change our presence. Humans cannot do this on your planet. You can change your makeup, hair color, and clothing, but it is only a superficial change. We can actually change the molecular structure of our essence by merely focusing new thoughts in creative light. We can also use frequency waves according to our will to make us appear as mere shadows, flickering lights, bright lights, or light bodies which you can actually see through, or more solid bodies similar to yours, but with an iridescent glow. Our forms consist of varying degrees of the color spectrum and light, for we are light beings and operate in the light. Our inner being, or the inside of our iridescent forms, is likened to a series of energy spheres like your chakras or electrical charges only we do not operate as an electrical body."

This was a difficult concept for me to accept, but I allowed my reality to be stretched.

"Now, you ask how do we think or communicate? In your case, you think, and so you are or become that which you think, and we can read your thought quite easily. In our case, we extrapolate thoughts that manifest in our universe, and then conform or redefine these thoughts. One day, in time, through your evolution, you, too, will be able to do some of these things as you move toward fourth-dimensional beings. We can hardly wait for that time, because we will be able to work with you side by side, more in attunement as our cosmic brothers and sisters.

"Already many humans on Earth are receiving our messages through their dreams, plays, books, and other inspirational paths. Our information is open to all humankind, not just a few. However, the information is given to only those individuals who are committed to doing the work with good intent, healing your planet, and are in service to humankind and to our Supreme Master of all Universes."

I did not ask Darius, but I wondered how many universes there were in the course of the heavenly order. I assumed there were an infinite number just as there are an infinite number of stars. Anyway, maybe later.

Darius seemed complete in his discourse. He parted in a loving blessing, saying that tomorrow I would meet another Blue Planet being named Zorus, who would continue with more information on the nature of the blue beings.

As we lay in bed that night, I remembered how unusual my husband, Bert, was, wondering which star system he was from. When I first met him, he carefully told me that he was different. He always had ample energy, never tiring, even though he was physically active much more than me. He was wise beyond the average human spiritual attunement, and always had answers when there seemed to be no answer. I told him some of the information I had been given regarding the Blue Crystal beings and he did not seem at all surprised. Although not directly experienced with them, he easily understood the concept of iridescent energy spheres and the ability to change form.

"You are providing a great service to the planet," he quietly said. "Just think how the average human will, on some level, begin to wake up, even if it is only on the subconscious level. It will be a start or a wake-up call that will be further awakened at some future event. This is true even if they are reading this only as a science fiction novel."

I nodded sleepily and drifted off into visions of unearthly hues of blue which I had not experienced in a conscious state and looked forward to my meeting with Zorus.

The next day the guides would not let me sleep, so I eagerly got prepared and began to type. Before I was introduced to Zorus, they encouraged me to get this material out as soon as possible, so that humankind would learn of the Blue Crystal Planet, Earth's sister planet and more about themselves and the universe or what you call the Cosmos.

Then, a radiant Being approached me at my computer. His fragrance and energy was different than that of Darius, but his light and spiritual beauty were of a similar Christ consciousness frequency. After a brief introduction, he asked my permission to speak, asking if he could give more information that was important for humans to understand. Rather than travel to the planet, he asked if he could simply relay information that would give more background to their goal of familiarizing humans with the Blue Crystal Planet, and I willingly consented.

"There are more topics that will interest the Earth beings, so shall we begin? First, I am called Zorus, and my name in your terms means 'one who has the knowing or knowledge beyond what you call your five senses.' We operate beyond the five senses, for we are not made of flesh and blood, but of an ethereal substance consisting of varying energy grids and light frequencies. Humans can also operate in their ethereal bodies and do so many times when they are not in their awakened or conscious state of being. However, this is more a reality than the illusion of self or the solid state of being in the physical vehicle. Unfortunately, many humans seem to be stuck in the mental state or mind in the physical form, but this will change to a more heart-centered, balanced state with time.

"It's like you drive a car which houses your physical body and transports you to whatever destination you want to go, but when you reach that destination, you leave the car and operate without it. In other words, you are conscious both in your physical body, and also leave it for other realms frequently in daydreaming, sleep, creative thinking, and so on. You are in and out of your physical body many times throughout the day.

"Please understand that your physical forms are a wonder for us to behold because they are the image of the God source. They are much more complex than a car, however. The physical form houses the soul that is connected to all living things and, therefore, has the God seed within. The soul does drive the body such as the physical aspect drives the car. The soul is encoded and programmed in such a way that it creates the life force that the physical form has. The DNA is the identity code and individualizes the body. This program is what operates the body and the many organs and cellular structures within.

"You probably think of us as being machines and not of the physical realm, however, it is the soul being that is the real nature of the Life Force. Since we all have souls which the Great Creator gave us, then we can choose what vehicle we wish to inhabit for a time. In Earth time it is measured in years, but in our reality, it is measured by increments.

"Now, when there is imbalance or negative energy, this can cause disease and can contaminate the body and mind. So, it is important that you learn how to reconnect with your soul being within in order to reprogram or modify your state of being. In other words, you can heal yourselves by retraining the social mind so it can adhere to the original soul blueprint to bring about a healthy mind, body, soul connection. Many ask how this can be done.

There are as many ways and techniques as there are answers. When you are in an altered or meditative state you learn to tune in. Then the answers come easily and you do not have to use your brain to think, so to speak. You only have to use your intuitive powers and intuit this information such as you are doing now. Each of you is wired in your own unique way so there is no one way to do this. Some of you have success with hypnosis or past-life regression or future renderings. Others are able to tune into their soul being rather easily. This is why it is important for you to teach some of these methods to others so they can open their minds for acceptance of intuiting for themselves.

"We, on the other hand, operate on this level most of the time. We do not have to think in the way you would, for all we do is tune our frequency up or tune in, and we can telepathically communicate with our species. The beings see you in your true state of being, in your light body in which you are your true selves. If you could see this, you would be transparent. The Crystal species sees you as such, so they can move through your physical bodies and physical manifestations such as your buildings and forests and defy your gravitational pull. Their molecular structure allows them to do this. In time earthly beings will be able to do this as well. You do so much of this in your altered states or dream states and, as I mentioned, you are out of your bodies more than in.

"There is no concept of time or space on the Blue Crystal Planet; therefore, the beings that live there have the power to stop linear time or space on Earth. To understand how this might work, think of someone about to be in an accident and the blue beings put space and time in a holding pattern and prevent the accident from happening. Soon, humans will be aware of the ability to control time and space with thought.

"Now all you need to do is recognize these innate abilities, which are similar to ours, and bring them into your consciousness, and they will develop in due time. Know that this is not a new concept, for when you were created or seeded here in the Earth, you had these abilities. Remembering to think in the light is the key.

"While you have to deal with the physical body and its intricate parts, we do not, for we are an evolved species and operate in the electromagnetic paradigm. We are light and colors of varying frequencies. Encasing your physical bodies is your aura or magnetic energy. This is like a protective membrane or bubble that is impenetrable. So you see, you do have a likeness of us—your brothers and sisters, in that you are surrounded with electromagnetic energy and do have a light body. As we progress in this book, we wish to share with you more ways that you can adjust your being to the higher state or level, such as we speak of, and in time, operate in this higher frequency state rather than your physical bodies.

"As you know, Ethel, the author, is an intuitive. This is the reason that she can read people well. For it is that she aligns herself with the cosmic thought patterns, and is able to reorganize them in the form that can be accepted or communicated. This is an easy task for her to do for she had training to think in the light. This does give her problems with her physical body, as she sometimes feels shorted out. This is true in one sense, but not in another, for we will help her to allow the molecular structure to reverberate back into the necessary physical pattern. In the case of the Blue Crystal beings, on our plane we are all consciously intuitive.

"Now your text, the Bible, talks about sacrifice or sacrificing the lamb. That is a reference to sacrificing the physical body in order to release the ethereal form or the body that was intended in the first place. There was in the early stages of Earth evolving, adhering to or living in a physical body or even an animal body, so the soul did get stuck, so to speak, and forgot the God source connection; so thus, the evolution cycle began; but remember that it was not meant to be negative. However, because the soul became so encased and infused into animalistic form and solidity, it has and will take much time to recycle itself to its original state of the Adam and Eve that your text talks about.

"I know that this is more of a lesson in the creative process and events that led mankind into being what it is today, but it is important for you to realize the path you have taken. Also, we, as your planetary sisters and brothers, want to share this information about our differences and similarities and assist you with this knowledge. This provides you with the opportunity to modify and make the necessary changes to enlighten your species to bring it to higher levels and frequencies, and begin the process of redeveloping into fourth- and fifth- dimensional beings and operating in the light waves of universal energy.

"Your scientists have already been working on light waves and color for healing the body without invasive surgery or other medical techniques. It is time, and you will see the results. There are so many advances in science, religion, and the medical field that within the next few decades, you will already consider yourselves advanced beings. When you can do this and reprogram the mindset of mankind and weed out those that want to continue to dominate in a war-mongering way, then there will be much more peace and prosperity. More on this later.

"We thank you for communicating with us especially, at this early hour in your time. Keep in mind that we will continue to protect you and to work to remove your physical ailments. You will begin to gather more strength from the light and healing will take place and you will experience more energy in the physical body, and a more alerted mind as well, as we work together on this book.

"Much light and love and healing to you and yours. We are the guardians of light and we come in peace and love, for you are God's children, and you are our brothers and sisters."

With these loving blessings, Zorus ended this session. I felt his intense loving aura surrounding me all through the writing. My own frequency was raised to a brilliant radiance.

The next day, I reflected with Bert on the material I had received in the session spent with Zorus. Especially poignant was the reminder that time can be manipulated in a positive way when it became necessary. Years before, my son, Robert, and I actually witnessed such an event. When my daughter, Cherrie, was about five years old, she stepped off the sidewalk onto the asphalt of a grocery store parking lot. My son and I thought that she was behind us. We heard a screeching sound of the breaks of an oncoming car. Alerted by this sound, we turned around in time to see a beautiful angelic being pick her up and place her back on the sidewalk out of harm's way in front of the store. It happened in slow motion, and time was literally stalled for the instant it took to move Cherrie.

CHAPTER FOUR

Birthing and Life Processes on the Blue Crystal Planet

"You fear death because your conscious level is your dominant level
and the population in general is not accustomed to entering
and facilitating in the higher dimensions."

It seems that there is so much information the guides want to share with me and our world, that every day I that feel an increasing urgency to move forward with the material being given. Of course, there is no concept of time and space on their planet, so in the three-dimensional paradigm it's as if we appear to work in increments or intervals. In the timeless state they are always around even though I do not always perceive this. Their energy is always here and they are working on infusing and integrating positive love and light to the entire Earth as well as to me.

Darius appeared to me in brilliant white light and love as I offered time at the computer. He wanted to first describe the birthing process on the Blue Crystal Planet which certainly tweaked my interest, and I began typing after going into a trance state.

"On our planet, we do not operate as much like individual entities as the Earth species. We have a totally different way of developing and evolving, since we function on the fourth-, fifth-, and sixth-dimensional frequencies. When you are born, you have to choose, or rather your spirit chooses the physical vehicle in which you wish to develop. To us, the human life cycle, especially the birth and socialization process on Earth, is such a long and tedious task, as we see how children are born and develop in periods of growth, such as infant, child, adolescent, adulthood, and finally, into elderly species. Since they have a physical body or form, so to speak, they have to be continually nourished and fed, so they can maintain the life force and the physical body.

"You are just seedlings, so you have a different way of growth and evolving. It is a different way of life than on a planet of higher frequency. There is what you call death of the body, but not so with your soul being or spiritual part. It just changes form and space so it can operate as it was meant to be. This is what you would call the Reward of Heaven because once you release yourself from the physical body, you return to being a spiritual entity, which you have always been. It is interesting for us to watch this process, as it is quite alien to us.

"We procreate in a much different fashion. First of all, we are androgynous, but we do have a dominant sex in that we have use of our femininity or masculinity, depending on which we wish to express at any given time. The choice is agreed upon by two beings, but also decided on by the group with which we align ourselves.

"Next, we imprint ourselves with our own blueprint or what you call DNA, and the entire group is involved in the process of infusion and integration. It is a wondrous thing to see, and there is much light, power and love. In this process, the designed blueprint is then imprinted or manifested first in various colors such as you have never seen on Earth. It is given a type of form or light body in which to operate. There is also a purifying process that you do not have on your planet. This keeps our species in a more perfected state of being, and also a protected state of the life force that we have here.

"Our beings are not born like yours of flesh and blood, and skeletal frames or composition. They are created of Christ light and love. They are new in the sense of procreation, but they are already defined in other ways and levels. They are what you would call 'raised' by the whole of our species and their original parents are not owners of their new being, so to speak. They are what you would call adopted into our system. The parents are called custodians in your terms, and they are responsible for their learning, adjusting, adapting, and well-being. However, there is not this emotional attachment as there is with your species.

"They belong to the group and the whole of our vast system, and they are guided by many beings, teachers and guides. They are never alone, and they do not have the concept of fear or struggle. All of their needs are provided for from the first time they are created. This is a difficult idea for your species to grasp, but as we teach you more about ourselves, you will have a somewhat better understanding.

"We do have varying levels in which we operate or function. For instance, we have a type of school, but it is strictly voluntary. Those who want to advance or evolve come to various gatherings, and then, are imparted or infused with knowledge or wisdom. There are teachers here, too, but we call them interconnected beings or masters, for they interconnect our species with the universal or cosmic vision. Then, that information is infused within their being or within their high-powered conscious level which is a type of electrical system in their makeup.

"Once it is connected or infused, they will always retain it and have a way to reconnect to it in order to retrieve it. They do not have a memory system such as yours, and they know which circuits to recharge, so to speak. It is a type of information bank that is recorded, but to us is always restored at will. For you, it is not an easy task to recall because you have not learned to reconnect to all your circuits in the way that we do. When you learn how your brain operates in its various regions, then all you will have to do is learn the various regions and program yourselves to do this automatically. You will direct your thoughts then to Region A, so to speak, or Region B, which then can give you a road map to your brain and to the various circuits that connect to that area. It may seem complex to you now, but in the future it will be so easy for humans to access needed information.

"We also have what we call Adjusters or humans would call physicians. Our Adjusters perform similarly in the sense that they change, modify or replace our energy system. It is not that we are ill or diseased like mankind, but that we need adjustments or re-alignment from time to time. This balances or readjusts our systems just as humans correct their physical bodies by operations or remedial surgery. We are not perfected beings either, so we, too, need assistance from time to time.

"However, when we get our adjustments, we do not have to wait or make an appointment with a practitioner. It is done on an immediate basis by a group of Adjusters who are always on alert and ready as a need arises. They can read out our necessary signals and then telepathically call upon the group to come to our assistance. There is no pay or billing system such as in the Earth environment. It is our Heavenly duty to attend to those in need so we are there to do this at any given time. The one receiving help so appreciates it, that they send us light and love that also enhances our well-being. We are so grateful to do this kind of work.

"It would be beneficial if mankind could learn to assist in this manner as well. The best kind of service given is that of love and compassion without the need to be repaid in some way. All that is required is the exchange of love and light. Humans have yet to learn how to operate with this concept and to understand that when your Master Christ taught to love your neighbor as yourself, that is what He meant. It is our hope that someday your planet will choose to operate with this kind of love and that there would be no need for money in exchange for services. This will take a long time as there is greed and loss of soul connection among humans.

"The kind of service that humans have that is most similar to our free exchange of energy is the voluntary system where people actually offer their services due to their ability to put aside their ego and pride and choose to help others without the need to be paid. This is the closest we can come to explaining how we operate. This allows such a freedom for us in the sense that we work from our soul level and it is the most liberated that we can be. The Earth concept of freedom is far from the universal freedom that can be obtained. Humans cannot feel the kind of ecstasy we feel until they are on this level or at this pivotal point. In time this will be more comprehended, but we encourage humans to continue to work on this even at the point of light that they are expressing, so it can spread, however minimally, to enhance the light of others and of mankind everywhere on the planet.

"One major difference between your spiritual structure and ours is that the Blue Crystal beings do not judge themselves or each other. They understand themselves and do not take offense or have negative thoughts. They help each other advance and evolve without question. They all work for the betterment of each other as well as the whole planet. When they do get together they work as group souls and can manifest themselves at will. It is such a different concept than you have on your planet.

"Again, we have to emphasize that we are all ONE and not independent, separate entities as you perceive yourselves to be. This is why you need to have a feeling of belonging and you so attach yourselves to your parents and family and small groups of like kind. You are all one and part of the same tapestry or universe. You each have your own blueprint or DNA, so to speak, but you are all part of the whole. When you realize this, you will know that in order to live a more evolved life or work towards perfection, you will not have to rely upon yourselves as much as depend upon the entire species and environment. For without each other, you would not exist. This is still a main lesson that your planet has to learn."

Even though in trance, I interrupted Darius to ask, "Why is it that humans fear death and are not comfortable with the process of leaving the body to enter higher dimensions?"

"You fear death because your conscious level is your dominant level, and the population in general is not accustomed to entering and facilitating in the higher dimensions. When you wake up from your sleep so to speak, you will be more able to tune into the soul remembrance and know who, why, how and who you are. You only experience the physical level and your five senses because from birth the higher-dimensional openings were squelched by your parents and society in general. You fear death because you operate with only the five senses because you are only focused on the solidity of things instead of the illusion that you are.

"You see, you are much more than you deem yourselves to be. It's like you paint a canvas and only see that or what you paint. You live or exist only in the given focused moment instead of living and focusing on the other conscious levels that you possess. This is why your psychics are what you call intuitive, due to their ability and lack of fear, so they can focus on the past, present, and future at the same what you call time or simultaneously. But remember there is no time out there or space, as these are only the constraints of your mental knowing and consciousness that you are infused with. If you were to allow your mind and consciousness to wander you would experience many, many realities not just yours. This again is hard to explain because we have to use the tools of communicating that we have at this present moment.

"Now, as newborns, you come into this plane knowledgeable and wise. You come in with knowledge of all your past lives, experiences, and numerous talents and the soul contract you have agreed on for this life. Then, for most, when you come out of the womb, your real conscious level is shielded from the rest of your being for a time. This is to protect you and to safeguard your physical being until it is oriented and adapted to your many environments. Some of you bring your talents and knowledge and intuition with you from day one, while others allow this remembering or process to gradually occur over your Earth time. This is why you have protégées who play symphonies like Mozart and Beethoven. They know who they are from the beginning, and are aware, and not afraid to allow their mental consciousness to get in the way.

"If you were to, what you call hypnotize even infants, you would be surprised at what you would discover. They have a language of their own, and your species does not understand it, just like your animals have a language of their own which you still do not understand. But the many cries and movements of infants can be interpreted, if you should take the time to study and to make some sense out of them. This is very frustrating to the infant, for he knows what he wants or desires. This is an interesting phenomenon to observe on your part. The Blue Crystal beings can communicate with these entities, your children, for we do this with a read-out of their vibrations or voice intonations.

"Now, it is true that some scientists on Earth are discovering voice interpretations with a certain device and know what that person is saying. Well, if you were to study voice vibrations and frequencies of infants, you, too, would be able to receive a read-out. As they mature and grow, you try to teach them to talk. This is a difficult task, for they communicate in a better way similar to a telepathic line or wave length. It is a sound wave length that they use. Each sound puts out a vibration tone that could be linked to symbols. They do not speak in words or phrases as you do, but in tones that, once decoded, would be symbols that equate to the language of words that you have.

"In time, your species will develop a technical device that can decode many sound vibrations and be interpreted as a new communication method, just as you have done work similarly with the dolphins. This is critical work, for the dolphins have existed on your Earth plane for eons of time, and they have coded within their systems the evolution of the planet. Communication is a viable instrument, and humans have a lot to learn in the area of being able to talk with the animals or with your own species that do not use the same language as you do. The magnificent

Universe has its own language and we will give you more information on this topic later.

"So, how did the beings of planet Earth arrive at the condition you find yourselves in now? Why is there such a lengthy birth and growth cycle instead of almost instant creation such as we have? Humankind has free will, as do we and all creatures, and you chose to change and experiment with material matter, and that which was bestowed upon you by our Magnificent Creator. Thus, began the story of Adam and Eve. After the 'fall' into matter, humans began the eons-long journey to return to the perfected beings that you once were. You became a mutated species and chose to evolve through incarnations in the many life expressions, including your beloved animals, insects, birds and the billions of varying forms.

"Now you must continue to evolve your way back to perfection and adapt new ways to further refine the frequency of your species and return your planet to its original pristine condition. This is where we come in as do our other brothers and sisters of the many planets in your Universe. We all are called upon to share with you the many ways to change, infuse and integrate the energies of the fourth- and fifth-dimensional paradigms into your planet. New light waves of positive, healing energies are constantly being transmitted to your Earth.

"This, of course, will take more time because there is so much destruction and division among your species. However, we are here to take on the task and to assist you in any way. You are already beginning to take our advice and to clean up your environment and partake of the higher energies.

"There is actually great, mostly unrecognized advancement taking place behind the scenes, so to speak, and the Earth is experiencing incredible changes at an extremely rapid speed. We are now seeing the results of the amazing assistance of the White Brotherhood of the Ascended Masters and Christed beings from other planets. The Earth is in the midst of the required chaos which will result in changes in environmental care, corporations, schools, and any institution that does not practice love as its founding principle. It is exciting that we live in a time where the eons of evolution for many souls are coming to a climax. The opportunity for ascension where the physical body changes to a crystalline body, is now presenting itself during the time of 2012 and beyond. Those Earth beings who have cleared their karma and wish to move forward into the higher dimensions can now do so with the transforming energy entering our solar system. Much work remains to be accomplished for this to happen and our purpose here is clear."

In an instant I was aware of my office and surroundings. Darius bid me farewell, and I was enveloped in a frequency so high that I could hardly catch my breath. I sat motionless and waited for my body to be grounded into the Earth. I visualized branches growing from my feet into the center of the Earth and with the help of my guides I fully entered my physical body.

With high anticipation, I waited to tell Bert about the birthing process on the Blue Crystal Planet. That evening at dinner, I relayed the information I had received that day.

"It is such a strikingly different paradigm," he said. "However, I recall similar types of birth processes from my own experiences as I travel back to my home planet. It is often discussed that the Earth, up until recently, has been delayed in its evolutionary development. As you realize, Earth is one of the less highly developed planets in our solar system, and our lengthy socialization process is for some, quite painful to endure. What is particularly sad is that most children enter our planet wide open psychically, and then close down after age three or four because adults do not encourage or accept interaction with the other dimensions, like angelic playmates and so on."

I murmured in quiet agreement and remembered a case where a client of mine had been born totally open psychically and saw angels and loved ones on the other side and his parents had the church people come pray for him because they thought he was possessed, not understanding the significance of his gift. This totally destroyed his self-confidence in spiritual contact for many years.

"There are some enlightened parents now who accept that their children are born open," I offered. "They actually encourage contact with their child's guides and spiritual friends, and in those cases, the veil of forgetfulness does not fall in place."

"Let us pray that as more high-frequency people enter the earth, they will follow this example, so the child matures with his spiritual contact intact and his guidance active and useful," Bert responded, and sighed as he reached across the table for my hand.

I was so grateful that I was with such a highly developed being for my husband.

CHAPTER FIVE

A Tour of the Government Chamber, Communication Center, and Akashic Records

"Today, we are taking you on another tour of our planet. Sit back and relax, as it will be unlike any tour you have ever taken on your Earth."

The following day, I awoke unable to contain myself, as my curiosity about the Blue Crystal Planet was extremely heightened. I must have been anticipating the amazing journey I was about to embark on as I sat impatiently waiting at my computer. I centered myself in my heart and called on my personal guides and angels to calm and focus my thoughts. Soon several Blue Crystal beings, including Darius, appeared in an array of luminous golden light emanating a heavenly fragrance of flowers.

Darius looked at me—or rather through me—in a blaze of almost overpowering love. I simply sat and allowed the energy to enter my physical and spiritual bodies, and felt uplifted and at one with all the beings present.

A few minutes later he said, "Today, we are taking you on another tour of our planet. Sit back and relax, as it will be unlike any tour you have ever taken on your Earth."

I sat in great expectancy and joy, awaiting what was to happen. Immediately, I began to feel like I was floating on a cloud, and I felt quite light as if I had taken my outer clothing off. One of the guides informed me that my physical embodiment was cumbersome and would not do in their purified environment that I had just discarded.

"It's like you are in your dream state while in your physical body and can move about easily because you are moving in the light and with your mind only, so relax and take another journey with us," he coaxed. "Now, again, once you have been oriented here you will learn to soar in your light body and we can identify you easily because you still do not have the frequency that we operate on. However, as last time, you will be assigned a tour guide or, sometimes, several guides to assist you."

As I soared and swirled away, I had the astounding, accelerated feeling of taking in the whole picture at once. Darius continued, "You will see magnificent crystal buildings with this beautiful blue hue to them, unlike any you have ever seen. It is a magnificent light and sight to behold! You will think you have died and gone to heaven. Well, our planet is one of the heavens or mansions that your Christ spoke about. It is connected to the heavenly realms, although it is in alignment with your Earth which is why we call it your sister planet.

"As you saw briefly before in your earlier visit, the buildings are pyramid shaped, spiral, or sometimes dome shaped and are fully lighted with their own energy or crystal power. They look like diamonds in the sky. We can move through them just by changing our frequency, and each is coded and protected. The light from them is so bright, that you would not be able to see them with your physical naked eye, which is why we are with you every step of the way.

"Now, when you see with your light body, it will seem like a mirrored reflection to you for you cannot enter without changing your frequency. When you adjust, you will literally float through the crystal buildings and objects. As during your last visit, we will help transport you so you do not get stuck in a certain place due to the attractive joy of being there.

"As you move about, you will be floating, as if on wings. You will be able to distinguish varying lights and colors and, also, sounds that you cannot hear with the human ear. These sounds come into your light body and fill you with love and harmony. You may even feel a tingling feeling or pulsations within that you have not felt before. As when you traveled here the first time, there is also instant healing available, for should you have any type of physical disease or ailment, you will not have this anymore, for this healing comes through your ethereal body first, then translates and recodes your physical body. It would be like programming your computer and putting in a new disk. So it is with this process."

Darius continued, "First, we will visit our Governing Center or what you would call the capital city in your world. We, too, have a capital arena which radiates a brilliant gold color, such as your Christ mentioned when he referred to streets of gold. It gives off a frequency such as you have never seen before. This color exemplifies the highest intellect, and the beings here only use this intellect and wisdom to govern our planet and to be connected to other universes. It is a sight to behold! Now, along with these various differing frequencies, most of the beings look golden in appearance."

I observed the immense, shining, golden rays emanating from the buildings of this capital city, and I could barely focus on them more than a few seconds. My guide, seeing my difficulty, quickly adjusted my frequency, so I could withstand the radiating energy.

He stated, "We will take you to what you would call our Governing Chambers inside the capital. You will then be able to see our Community Access Chamber, which is like your Congress, where you may be able to witness the way we govern our planet."

With the assistance of Darius, I floated near a golden chamber and remained on the outside, yet seeing through the crystal walls. The first thing I felt was a totally non-threatening environment. It was like being in a bubble of light that enhanced love, understanding, and harmony. I noticed and felt no conflict or discord there, but varying opinions or decisions were being heard and resolved in a most unique way. My guide observed me as I took all this in.

He remarked, "We, too, have varying degrees of feelings and thoughts about issues, but a unique way of handling differing viewpoints. These beings only concern themselves with intellect and thought. You must be worthy to be in their presence and also invited, as you are today. These are the masters and scholars of Ancient Wisdom and Universal Knowledge. We must have permission to enter. It is similar to the Vatican in Rome where only certain of your people can enter the most holy of the holiest. So it is with this city, for it is governed by such entities, and they are Holy Sacred Ones."

I saw many individuals focusing together in mutual love and respect, and I sensed that their manner of interacting supported each other in ways our planet had never experienced.

These buildings looked so complex to me that they only took me to a few more to have a quick glimpse of what they were about and how they operated. This place was quite far advanced and most of the other ordinary inhabitants of the planet did not even enter. These highly developed beings of the Governing Chamber report back to the High Council or their governing body, and this information is shared with the public, who are all invited into the great halls for that purpose.

Next, I found myself simply reclining by a beautiful diamond pool of unearthly hues of blue and gold hue. Darius remained with me, and since I still wanted to just rest, I decided to ask some questions. "I know you do not use speech like we do, but can you clarify more about how the inhabitants communicate with each other here and with the other planets in the universe?"

Darius replied, "It would be necessary for you to visit our spiral city which is our Communication City or Chamber. Would you like to go now?"

I felt new energy surge around my body and enthusiastically floated up in response. I was zoomed higher towards a city or gathering place of transparent buildings of a spiral structure or architecture. Every build-ing either spiraled up or down or sideways, unlike any configuration I had ever seen. I paused while suspended and tried to comprehend the overview, which was amazing. The buildings were not so much different colors, but of varying hues, and, when I would pass them from overhead, I heard different sounds or tones emitting from each. They were not in a row, but overlapping somehow without touching or invading the space of the next one. Some had many winding configurations while others were simple. Darius described how various levels of each spiral were con-nected to different parts of the universe or other universes. It was like a million helixes all rolled into one.

I was told that this was the Communication Chamber of Masters who were multitasking and not only worked on projects for their planet, but worked directly with other celestial bodies and even universes. In addition, their responsibilities included communicating current infor-mation to the beings on their planet as well. These masters emitted quite a brilliant luminescence that reflected several dimensions or layers. It was enormously evident that they differed from the average being on the planet. Their auras were fully extended and appeared to me to be huge or vast compared to other beings I had observed. Their responsibilities and areas of expertise were markedly more complicated than other workers.

As he led me inside one of the spiral buildings, Darius explained that while there was a Universal language, there were several ways of communicating between heavenly bodies. I was able to witness a few for myself, which he kindly explained to me in terms that I could just begin to understand.

He began, "One type of communication is using sound only, and this includes variations of themes or topics. A group of sounds comes in blocks and then sometimes pauses, and then another group appears in waves and blocks. We have types of highly technical machines that decode intonations into symbols so we can better understand. These sounds usually do not resonate like any kind of words or even music on the Earth, but I will let you experience them so you can judge for yourself. Moreover, many forms of our communication are not possible to hear with the human ear. Sometimes they would be like a foreign language to you, or a kind of tapping or Morse code. Other times they come in a type of lettering or configuration on a screen, but they would appear rapidly, not word by word, but by pages. This is similar to an amplified version of your computer, but more highly technical. Some of our communication is carried out in colors and waves."

As he spoke, I turned in every direction to observe the machines he referred to and the cacophony of signals, colors, and symbols. There was focused attention in a calm, orderly manner.

"We communicate with other planets in the universe and exchange information and knowledge. Part of this information is used to plan our visits to other planets and their journeys here. We have a unique bond with these many different planetary beings and consider ourselves members of a diverse universal culture and treat each other with the utmost respect. We have a special place where space beings land and great halls where they are greeted and hold meetings for a variety of interplanetary cultures."

Such phenomenal information was coming to me! I would be totally overwhelmed to be present at such a gathering, but maybe later....

Meanwhile, Darius provided examples of intonations that might sound familiar to me. Information came in waves and an oscillating form of a sort, and some had the most beautiful colors which I cannot describe as they were just too awesome for words. I was not able to discern any sounds that were actually intelligible to me.

Then my guide continued, "Now, there is a method of communication between individuals using our light bodies, where we have a type of integration or infusion with each other and a blending of energies. In your world, you would greet a person with a hug or kiss. Here, sometimes we just blend energies and you feel our presence throughout your entire mind, body and soul levels. Not only that, you would get a message given to you about, perhaps, something you have been working on or thinking about, or you may need a type of readjustment, healing, or cleansing. This is known immediately, for we can read your desires or needs or perhaps observe that you just want validation or affirmation. So, telepathically, you would receive love, healing, and communication. Isn't that a remarkable thing? You humans are required to think out things or thoughts and communicate in verbal sounds that resonate with the other person.

"Another phenomenon here is the ability to do a complete readout of the person on an immediate basis, yet you will not see us move our lips or talk in sounds. We emit messages in a totally different way. You will actually see sound waves floating and taking form, and you can hear with your inner Being, rather than your ears. There are a multiplicity of frequencies and varying colors that match up with the sound intonations. Likewise, each color has its own sound wave and frequency. It is a beautiful sight to behold. It is interesting to note that on Earth there are sounds humans cannot hear, but your animal creatures pick up easily. This is somewhat related to what we do.

"When you observe us with your ethereal light body that can pick up these frequencies, you will have to sort of do a double take. You will see a beautiful color form that can change in the blinking of an eye, because we have the ability to change quickly. So, ask our guides to help you maintain the image in your cosmic mind and to put it on hold like you would a movie frame to pause and retain, so you can better comprehend what you see."

I did not mind exiting this chamber, for it was so complicated even for my ethereal cosmic mind that I could not comprehend it at all. I was glad to move on and several other guides joined us. They could tell that I was totally exhausted and needed a rest. They began to work to balance my energies and my mindset and I felt as if I were almost tranquilized. They, of course, had to get my permission to work on me in this way on my own time and at my own speed. These beings did not urge or force me to do what I did not desire to do. They gave me many options for rest, and let me make my own decisions. They have that kind or respect and humor. If I did not want to continue, they lovingly told me they would then assist me to return to my Earthly home and would guide me all the way. These beings are the kindest and most thoughtful I have ever encountered, and that includes those on the Earth as well. They say that one of the things that they do not want to do is to interfere with my own free will. I have a profound love for them, as they emanate an unconditional caring, and the only way I could describe it is that they are truly Godlike.

They had so much to show and share with me that I received this incredible feeling of attachment and devotion, although they told me they do not want humans to worship them, but only to respect and honor their souls as they honor ours. You see, humans are comparably in the infant state of being, whereas, the Blue Crystal beings have experienced timelessness and higher-dimensional life. Since we are in the process of learning to advance toward their level of development, it is almost natural to be in awe of them. Their souls, for instance, have experienced many, many universal systems, while ours have experienced only some. We, also, are caught in a web of Earth evolution, as well as soul evolution, and we must experience many lives on Earth for our soul's learning before we experience other universes and dimensions. Some humans do astral travel to these other places, and, yes, we do originate from various outer limits which we call our home base, but we all do not have this experience of advancement.

I chose to rest and seemed to be reclining in a unique sort of way. I could feel my ethereal body as very light and expansive. However, when I was in a state of repose here it was as if I had collapsed or literally unfolded into myself, and, when I was shown a reflection of myself, I actually laughed because I looked so funny, like an accordion closed up, yet, in such a relaxed state, I felt like jelly. I didn't want to move or even get into another kind of state for this was pure joy and so serene. I don't know how long I rested, but it felt as if I were a baby in a cradle or were cradled and immersed in love. They did not have to wake me up, I just opened up as you would expand your consciousness, and I unfolded and maintained my ethereal form again.

In a more refreshed state, I began to ponder another question. "Please help me to understand and be able to communicate to the Earth humans exactly what you look like so they can picture you and hold your form in their minds."

"We are a type of angelic form, not with arms and legs, but with bands of color and energy that would appear to you like wings. Each of us differs slightly in accordance with our so-called level of being and heavenly profession, so to speak. For our legs you would only see a type of sphere connection which is the way we transport ourselves here and throughout other dimensions. They would appear like rolling spheres in a circular motion. Our heads look circular like yours, but are often in motion because we can move about at will to see all things at once. You would have to move your head or turn around to see behind you, however, we do not. We only circulate, or a better explanation is that we put our cosmic minds and heads in connection with a full motion to capture all that is around us, be it in front, side, or behind, in your terms. Remember that there is no such thing as direction or space in our world, but we manipulate and ride the sound waves or magnetic electrical fields and beyond."

I thanked him and felt as if I were just beginning to grasp a whole new and unbelievably amazing way of expressing life in our immense universe. My heart overflowed with the joy of simply being in the presence of these beings. I had so much to learn and could hardly absorb what I was experiencing because it was all so attractive and new. The energy was persuasive and I felt such a longing to know more, to understand and experience an entirely different paradigm, far, far, beyond planet Earth. And it was all so immensely beautiful.

Darius seemed to be easily reading my thoughts.

"Yes, there is still so much more to show you! I would like to take you to a most fascinating chamber before you return to Earth and that is the Hall of the Akashic Records."

I eagerly consented, and was immediately swirled up into a vortex and was shown a place of all recorded information about creation, other worlds, dimensions, and Earthly lives. Everything is recorded in these Akashic Records or the Book of Books that our Master, the Lord Jesus Christ, taught us about. I was told we can access these records at any time, but it had to be with good intent and purpose of knowledge and wisdom that we gain from the information. It was explained to me that everything that is, has been, or will be, is coded in our Soul Seed. What an intriguing fact to know!

As I entered these chambers, I found that it was easier than going to our Earthly libraries or computers. Their histories were on a type of disc, but unlike those we have on Earth so far. It seemed to be made of crystal and was composed of an unknown material. It glittered with energy bands of light infused with numerous colors unknown, as yet, to man. Once a person is granted access to these records, his mind is literally opened for easy reception and understanding. One does not actually read these records as we do on Earth, because it is a universal type of language that one can immediately comprehend and understand. It was a holograph of vision, sight, sound, feelings, and memories that came at me all at once. There was no division, but instead, a blending of thoughts that literally became things or are manifested in such a way that it was effortless to grasp. This is what was meant by the statement, "You will understand it by and by when you reach the heavenly realms."

Darius explained that when one receives this valuable information, it is up to him to do with it what he desires. There is always salvation available and assistance for those who need to contemplate their misdeeds or what one calls the sins of the Earth.

"One does reap what he sows, and he will find many opportunities to find his way in the Divine Plan that he inherited when he incarnated into the Earthly plane, as well as other worlds. One does have his heavenly guides and teachers to assist him, but they will only give suggestions, not demands that one do such and such."

He continued, "Can you imagine what it would feel like to sense or use all of your senses at the same time plus your cosmic senses as well? We can only give you the analogy of seeing, sensing, feeling, hearing all your Earthly experiences at the same time. Well, it is much easier to do this in a given situation and to experience it in time increments. It is difficult to understand this with your Earthly brain, but more so with your mind. Now, expand that to include your cosmic mind. In your dream sleep state you have only bits and pieces that, somehow, do not make sense to your brain."

I awakened to Earthly consciousness and grounded myself again, I was back, and I was perplexed as to how I could possibly convey to humans what I had just experienced.

CHAPTER SIX

A *Tour of the Cosmic Academy and Chamber of Intellect*

*"Each city or gathering place had different lights and colors
to distinguish it from others."*

Two days passed as I absorbed the experiences of the last tour. The following night I awoke out of a deep sleep, feeling the presence of Darius, who was inviting me to join him. Soon, I was floating with ease with him beside me showing the way. We seemed to stop in the outer atmosphere of the Blue Crystal Planet.

He asked me if I would like to see a kind of map, so I could decide which destination I would like to experience next. He pulled up a version of a cosmic map which at first looked like a huge screen that had no dimensions to it and was like a hologram that moved towards me. Then he decided to simplify it and showed me a similar map of just his planet.

From outer space, it looked like a blue crystal ball, only it was gigantic in size compared to our Earth. Then he brought it down to a simpler flat sort of map that was still holographic. The Blue Crystal Planet just sparkled like a zillion stars in the vastness of space. It had many moons and suns that are not seen from our Earthly vantage point. There is no darkness, only light in varying degrees. The moons are as bright as the suns, but have a different purpose and are reflected. This map was sort of waving in front of me like a flag in the wind, because he had difficulty in pausing it for me to visually see with my ethereal eyes.

There were points of light on a grid that reminded me of what I see when I am in my altered state doing readings. Each city or gathering place had different lights and colors to distinguish it from others. Whereas Earth maps have different shapes and sizes with geographical names, theirs are distinguished by their colors of light, brightness, and reflections.

As I observed this strange map I noticed that their cities are not up and down like ours or directional like north south, east, or west, but positioned in varying patterns that I could not identify, like colored threads woven in a type of tapestry. I asked to be drawn to the lights that would fulfill my purpose for this visitation. I connected to the flow of varying energy grids and sensed a magnetic pull to the ones that attracted me. It was similar to Earthly travel maps highlighting places of interest, only this map had a targeted destination built into it.

This was an individualized map for me, and I could request to be shown the city that was for my highest good at the present. I found myself attracted to an area of varying hues of yellow that I later discovered was the Cosmic Academy.

As I looked at this map and the blazing lights coming from all directions, I became curious about how they organized their buildings, their cities, their culture. In my previous visits I noticed immense activity, constantly changing colors, fragrances, and sounds that were most overwhelming, yet, there seemed to be precise order.

So, I asked Darius, "Please tell me more about how this planet is organized or designed; it appears so orderly, yet there is constant motion, constant change."

Darius replied, "I think you will understand better if I take you to one of our work abodes so you can tour it for yourself and get a better idea of what we are about. Let us get permission to enter the Cosmic Academy. We will enter a type of code.

"However, first, we must prepare your ethereal body and cleanse and clear all preconceived thoughts and debris from your physical or mental being. We use a soft light energy to go through your light body so as not to shock you, and to give you a type of protective membrane that will sustain you. As we enter this beautiful area, you can see the yellow and white golden hues around everything here. You can get a bird's eye view, for you are above this gathering place. You can see the tall crystal buildings where they work, and as you look around more, you can catch a glimpse of their homes surrounding the city in a circular path. There are no streets or walkways or cars here because we can transport ourselves on the sound waves. When we go to other destinations, outside our dimension, then we use another mode which we will discuss later."

We were greeted by Orious, who is a Master Teacher and Guide of the Third Universe and lives in the Cosmic Academy. He allowed us to enter and visit, saying, "Welcome to our humble destination. First, I will lower your frequency rate so that I can use a decoding process in order to put visual pictures in your mind. Where would you like to begin or start the tour? You are a bit confused, because you have not been here before, and it's as if you are in a foreign land. So, I will take you in small steps and increments to explain to you what this Cosmic Academy is all about.

"First, you will not see any books or written materials. This is only used on your planet and a few others. Here, all is in symbol form through light and sound waves. We have various machines that you have never seen before. They are a type of advanced computer system. Here, we do not need to see things in pictures or visually, for we have created a way to form thoughts in waves that are then pictured in your mind using telepathy and our method of communication. Everything is stored in these telecryptic types of machines, which are based on codes. One letter or code could put out information, for example, of a lifetime of an individual or group of souls. It is somewhat difficult to explain, because it is beyond third-dimensional concepts. However, I will ask mentally if you would like to know your Earth purpose and give you that information immediately on a readout."

I nodded and was immediately given a mental impression that explained concisely my purpose for being on the Earth which included authoring this book about their planet. This was totally amazing, and I got the sense that they were technically unbelievably advanced. They did not see things in pictures or visually, but simply communicated their thought forms telepathically. Part of their communication included the ability to hold images in their minds for long periods of time.

Orious then described the type of work that he and others did in this chamber by bringing up a cosmic map of our universe and the various planets on a screen as a starting point of reference. He said that in a future visit he would provide a pictorial view and more information about our universe as it was a lengthy and involved topic.

However, he did explain briefly, "We have the history of our planet, as well as the Earth planet and other cosmic structures. We retrieve information from other planets, galaxies, and universes in the heavenly realms. We also teach others how to do this and how to use this information for their well-being and to their highest good. Knowledge is important, and its uses and application are even more important. Earth beings have forgotten their past and are lost in a way, but can reconnect to their soul seed, and with great effort return to their previous high frequency.

"You, Ethel, are contributing to this at this time, as the valuable information you are receiving is needed for the Earth to progress and pull itself out of the place it has been stuck for ever so long. You will assist your planet with the right tools to progress forward, and the beings from our planet will be at their side should they desire it."

I smiled in acknowledgment of the compliment, but the possibility of conveying to humans all that I had experienced with any kind of accuracy seemed out of the question at that time.

Orious proceeded further on the tour. I was transported to various rooms or chambers that were not so divided as here on Earth, but more a continuous stream of light or paths. It seemed so strange for me to ride on this wave without fear or apprehension. I had only a feeling of comfort and being embraced by light and love as I had never felt before. I really did not want this continuous joy to leave me.

Next, I floated through a chamber where I saw copper- or yellow-hued beings gathered in groups, each intent on the work that they were doing. Some seemed to be receiving information from strange types of machines emitting crystal lights or forms. Information came in streams of light and color, and at times I heard sounds that were comforting to my soul.

As I floated about, I saw another chamber that went sort of downward. I felt a lowering of my vibration or frequency, and spiraled downward into a pure golden light, where I saw copper beings doing a type of creating or manipulation. Then, I saw more clearly what they were doing. Oh, my goodness! They helped to manipulate the energies surrounding our planet, and to bring about smoothing energies that could stop earthquakes, hurricanes, tornadoes, and cataclysmic events.

I got the thought that they were doing God's work of trying to assist our planet and its nature forces to prevent destruction to mankind. This is what their purpose was and the work that they were assigned to do on behalf of humankind. The master here told me telepathically that he and his soul sisters and brothers requested to do this specialized work. Here were these wondrous beings on our sister planet, as well as other legions of angelic beings that were working together to bring about energy balances and to better align the planet, so it could stay on course and evolve in its spiritual path as intended from the beginning of time.

The master allowed me to see this process, so I could return to Earth and bring this information into conscious awareness and heighten the knowledge of what we, as humans, could do to help ourselves to save our planet. Yes, we were on course to make the necessary changes such as many environmentalists were doing at this very moment. We know we have help from outside ourselves, and we must honor those who are assisting us. These beings have chosen to work with the Earth's magnetic energy fields in bringing them in alignment and shifting the course of evolution. He told me that we must have the faith that the inhabitants of the Blue Crystal Planet were God's helpers and assistants who worked with us.

The master pointed out that when we exit or leave our human bodies, our souls have numerous opportunities in other dimensions to work on varying levels to advance and to assist others as well. Just as we have the free will and desire to assist the poor or less fortunate while on Earth, they, too, can do this from what we call the Other Side. They told me in time we, too, will learn that there is no such thing as the Other Side, only other waves of light.

He continued the tour, "Now that you have seen this, let us take you to another area called the Chamber of Intellect, which is similar to a school on your planet. This reflects the varying levels or frequencies on which we operate. This chamber is more of a white light with beautiful pastel colors of the rainbow like you see on Earth. The dominant color, again, is golden yellow, but it contains varying frequencies of the yellow light spectrum."

After a pleasant clearing procedure similar to that of the Cosmic Academy, we continued toward the Chamber of Intellect.

I saw a group of beings that seemed to be collecting information similar to a library on our Earth. There were many streams of light coming into each one's field or aura.

The master explained, "The light streams do vary in degree of knowledge, yet to you observing this, it seems the same. There are many levels of knowledge stored here, and it is preserved in a unique way. There are actual pockets of differing colors and sounds in their cosmic minds that represent knowledge, and you will be able to see this. They can retrieve information easily by varying symbols that they know. It's so easy, like punching a computer key, and it appears. They take this information and store it within and when they want to share it with others, they just think in a stream of light, and you can see it flowing out and connecting to another student or connecting to a type of machine of light that stores it as well.

"Those who want to advance or evolve come voluntarily to various gatherings here, and then are imparted or infused with knowledge or wisdom. There are teachers here, too, but we call them interconnected beings, or masters, for they interconnect our species with the universal or cosmic vision. Then, that knowledge is infused within their high-powered, conscious level, which is a type of electrical system in their makeup. Once it is connected or infused, they will always retain it and have a way to reconnect to it in order to retrieve it. They do not have a memory system like yours; however, they know which circuits to recharge. It is a type of memory bank that is recorded, but it is always restored at will. For you, it is not an easy task to recall because you have not learned to reconnect to all your circuits in the way that we do. When you learn how your brain operates in its various regions, then all you will have to do is learn the various regions and program yourselves to do this automatically. For example, you will direct your thoughts then to Region A or Region B, which then can give you a road map to your brain and to the various circuits that connect to that area. It may seem complex to you now, but in the future it will be easy to access this information."

I was instructed to transport myself by floating to other levels and sections of the Academy where various projects and work were in progress on a continuous basis. I asked if and when they need to rest. They responded that they can make adjustments to their bodies and modifications which do give them a type of recharge. They do not work continuously for days or weeks, as they are not on a linear time concept. They do have periods of rest and recreation and time to be with their families and soul brothers and sisters. They do complete a task or project in its entirety and do not have the need to come back to continue working on

it as we do. I will learn more of this later. Right now, it is very complicated in my Earth mind, but not in my cosmic mind.

I could have remained much longer, but my guides told me that I
must rest, so as not to exceed my energy levels. I spiraled outwards and
quickly found myself in another destination, where I saw a type of reclining furniture which I could see through even though it appeared solid
in form. I was instructed to lower my frequency and to allow my mind
to drift back to a familiar place on Earth where I would rest my body.
I sent out a thought form of a lovely soft and comfortable recliner and
lowered myself in it. I felt that I was home, and I went into a deep sleep
surrounded by love and protection with my angel guides.

As I rested, I heard the voice of Darius say, "You are now reprogrammed and are disease free. This has been a wonderful happening for
you, and you will come back to Earth as a new, revived person."

I returned consciously to my computer with Bert lovingly looking at
me. He had been standing in the doorway of my office for some time
observing and assuring himself that I was protected and returning to
my body safely. When I was fully grounded into the Earth, I rested for
several hours in bed and rejoined Bert for a late lunch in our kitchen. I
had so much to tell him and I was very excited.

It was difficult to put into words the adventures I had just experienced. He was, as always, interested and curious, asking many questions and trying to help me express in words the concepts I could only
begin to communicate. When I was discussing the Cosmic Chamber and
mentioned the copper beings, he became quite agitated and animated,
jumping up and nearly knocking over his coffee. "Ethel, Ethel, stop,
stop! Don't you remember the copper being that visited you when you
were channeling in our living room in Maryland with your friend, Jane? "

I did remember well, but I had not yet related that experience with
where I had just been with Darius. At the time Bert was referring to, I
was channeling with another person present whom I called my conductor. Her job was to ask questions while I temporarily left my physical

body and with the protection of my angels and guides, allowed master teachers, like Jesus, to use my voice and speak their truth to help others. I rested on the couch with my eyes closed while my conscious self-rested in a higher realm. My voice and speech would change and sometimes even my face would take on a hint of the form of the person speaking through me.

This particular time I was coming out of a session, and my eyes were open. Suddenly, a tall copper female materialized in front of us. She had a pointed head, copper eyes, and what appeared to be hard, copper scales over her entire humanoid body. She was not particularly attractive as a female, but she emanated a sweet, loving, and compassionate radiance. She came over to me and I reached out to her and my hand passed through her body and, surprisingly, I realized the scales were soft as feathers.

She said "I want to feel what it is like to have human emotion." She asked me to think of something sad, and I thought of my father dying when I was eleven years old. All of a sudden, tears came down her face, and she was very delighted that she could feel emotion and thanked me and blessed both of us and disappeared right before our eyes. Of course, we both could hardly believe what we had just seen.

Bert remarked, "That was so amazing, but, apparently, many life forms from other star systems do not experience the level or kind of emotion as humans do and come to our planet to learn and feel what they are like. It is a desirable attribute that we take for granted and sometimes people misuse and exploit negative emotions such as deliberately generating fear in the name of greed or control."

CHAPTER 7

A Dialogue with Darius on Emotions and Thinking

*"If humans chose to immediately reprogram an undesired emotion
and modify it for a better outcome, then they could easily move
on to a different higher frequency level which would quickly
bring about positive results or changes to all mankind."*

The next day I rested and relaxed, wanting to relish in the experiences of the previous tour. However, sometimes I felt like I was literally pushed or shoved towards my computer, and this was the case as I was awakened at 3:30 a.m. the following day with an urgency to continue writing this important manuscript so that people on Earth can know more about their sister planet. Darius was present and seemed to know what was on my mind.

As I fell asleep that night, I reminisced about the copper being who wanted to experience emotion as we know it. Darius began to speak.

"One of the things that the beings from the Blue Crystal Planet are learning from the human species is more about emotion for they can sense it in quite different ways. When we experience your kind of emotion, it literally jerks us or gives our light bodies a type of electrical shock, so we must be quite careful. We have to lower our frequency levels in order to adjust to the experience. When humans express a feeling, it is based on what they think or past memories which they hold on to and dwell on. Since we can control our thinking because we do not think like you, we can eradicate past negative memories. We have the ability to change or modify our thoughts in ways that you have yet to learn.

"For example, let's say that a human thinks of something hurtful that a friend or family member said to him. He remembers it and goes over and over the experience and puts so much energy into it that it becomes a living ethereal entity known as a thought form. There comes a point when he can actually see or visualize the manifestation of that feeling, and it lingers with him for moments, hours, and days. It can consume and control him, and, if played over and over like a CD, it manifests in ways that actually become stumbling blocks. Thus, a thought generates an emotion, and this results in a desire to express or release in the manner that he chooses such as anger, sadness, anxiety, or confusion.

"He may express his emotions by hitting an object in anger, or crying due to sadness, or becoming sick due to anxiety and numerous other manifestations that demonstrate the result of the feeling. When we observe humans expressing in this manner, we can actually see streams of various light frequencies emitting from their bodies, and it takes on a kind of form by which we can distinguish the colors and intensity. Currently, they carry too much of these emotional energies or charges, and this keeps them from moving forward toward their spiritual growth. It is as if they are caught in a web of ethereal substance and can't pull themselves out of it. However, it is important to experience the feeling, but then release the thought that connects with it as soon as possible in order to avoid getting stuck in that mode. Suppressing the emotion only delays dealing with it; discharge must occur at some time, hopefully, before resulting in illness or an energy blockage.

"We would like to teach humans how to release the connected emotional thought pattern and replace it with a positive and cleansing technique. There are many books and CDs on your planet that would reinforce this on topics such as relaxation, meditation, nature sounds, and hypnosis. Or they can simply listen to beautiful music.

"On a daily basis, the easiest way is to connect with their guides or the God within and ask for assistance to delete the negative thoughts that seem to control their lives. Unfortunately, this control is also reinforced by your news media, which dwells on negative factors, so appropriate choices in that area are called for. When one is going through a more severe emotional crisis, he can ask for Cosmic Light, or the Divine Light which aids in bringing the emotional body into harmonious alignment with the other bodies, including the ethereal, astral, and physical counterparts.

"In general, it would be helpful for humans to remember that they tend to recall and dwell on the negative emotions more than the positive ones. Negative thoughts will spiral out and rebound in stronger waves, which is why they have such strong emotions connected to them. Positive ones are the reverse and do not rebound in the same way.

"Also, there are other helpful methods which can be incorporated into the daily lives of humans such as in the workplace and in the schools. A five-minute pause or activity break encouraging all to be in a meditative or peaceful state is an effective way to encourage the release of negative energy. By doing this, those present come together as one, and each contributes to the betterment of the group. It is like a gathering of people praying together, but in a calm and silent manner. This would bring about more peace, and a healing to all that participate.

"One of the more destructive emotions that Earth beings experience is around fear and survival issues. We encourage humans to know that there is nothing to fear, but fear itself and that they can survive safely in an environment that is traditionally thought of as frightening. Even in the presence of wild animals, this can be accomplished because if one truly believed that he no longer had to fear them and chooses to emit the love frequency, the animals would just turn and go their way. Should one be confronted by, say, a bear or tiger, just stand still and telepathically send out all love and understanding, with no fear present. That animal will turn and go back to where he came from in an instant. This type of thinking and emotional control can be developed over time, and it can be tested on dogs or other creatures that are encountered with quite pleasing results. Remember the story of Daniel and the lions' den. God told Daniel not to fear them and he assisted in his reprogramming, and the lions just walked away.

"If humans chose to immediately reprogram an undesired emotion and modify it for a better outcome, then they could easily move on to a different, higher-frequency level which would quickly bring about positive results, or changes to all mankind. For example, let's say a person becomes angry with a coworker because of his behavior or actions. Immediately, he can reprogram or reassess the situation and allow himself to experience that feeling. Then, he can begin to dissipate the negative-thought process and replace it with a higher understanding of what took place and send out the love vibration with so much love that it overrides the negativity. This sends the negative emotion out into the ethers to dissipate and dissolve, never to return and results in what is called forgiveness. The brain can actually be reprogrammed to forget this particular situation or encounter, and can store the energy of the event in a personal delete file to never appear again. This technique can be understood and entered into the memory banks of humankind. Once this is taught and practiced time after time and repetitively, as is required for your species, they will begin the process of recalling their soul's destination and the divine light beings that they truly were when they were first created or reborn into the physical by God.

"The same phenomenon of building a negative thought form can be used to create a desired positive outcome. The method is the same—engaging in a feeling or desire repeatedly. First, replace any emotions that are destructive or harmful with positive, kind desires. This, then, allows one to align with all the other positive frequencies and join all the other beings who are doing likewise, which creates a continuum in the planetary grid. Believing in and focusing on building a utopia on planet Earth by continually reemphasizing the positive energies, and peaceful and harmonious outcomes, will result in its gradual creation. For it is paramount to never give up or give in to the lesser energies because creation follows, or is driven by thought in your physical world.

"This is why it's important to pray or meditate in numbers in a state of oneness, as it creates a more powerful volume of energy. Of course, it's important to pray or contemplate individually, but it becomes more powerful to use the light energy in a group of individuals, which is one of the reasons you have created your churches and religions to bring souls together to worship or give thanks in a group. This is fine, but it would be immensely more effective with purer minds, hearts, and souls. The thinking or static from the group of minds interferes with the flow and connective process. If you would float out of your physical state and look down with your ethereal bodies and sight, you would see the many disrupting lines and cross lines that interfere with the flow and the unity. The closest you come to the wavelength of oneness that carries the spark of God is when you all recite in unison, sing, or play instruments.

"We would like to share some knowledge about our ways and discuss some techniques we learned eons ago. One difference between our beings and humans is the method by which thoughts are stored in the human memory banks. Your brains operate entirely differently from ours which has to do with the way it was designed and the double helixes that encompass the brain and DNA. Ours is of the twelve-helix system, which encompasses not only our brain function, but also the extended cosmic mind bank that stores all memory from various lifetimes, forms, and universal knowledge. We have learned to access this on the conscious level. We have learned the universal code as well as our own personal code that is similar to the one that is imprinted on your individual and group soul seeds.

"Your species has become disconnected and does not recall the cosmic mind or plan, except that which you can recall in short form or in sporadic moments. You are still searching for what and who you are while we know what and who we are and how we connect to all things in the great universe. You can learn to extend your brain power, which, in turn, can extend your cosmic universal power from the Great God Source. It was not meant for mankind to be separated from the Source of all, but in the evolution of things, there was a great tremor from the heavens that was to pull all planets in alignment. Somehow, there were those of your galaxy that did not come into this cohesion and became separated from the main source of life and connectedness. Then, there had to be some type of evolutionary plan to retrieve those unfortunate planets to bring them back into alignment with the main universe.

"Your Master Christ taught many truths about your world and the God of the universe. He could only teach on an elementary level, so that mankind could receive some kind of understanding. This is the main reason he taught in parable form. When he spoke about the sheep and bringing them into the fold, he was referring to the planet being brought back into the fold or the universal alignment, so humans could commune with the Father directly and see Him face to face.

"Now, with the numerous ways of progressing and evolving, life after life, the soul can advance to its rightful place in the universe. Once humans cross over and are able to see through the veil or membrane that keeps the Earth intact, they will discover their true selves and become the advanced beings they were designed for in the first place. The Earth is in a type of bubble, as are humans, and once humans have plugged into their true selves, they will understand all things and will unite with others as One such as your Master Christ exemplified.

"Humans will live in an environment that is free of negative energy because they can discern and begin to identify it. Once they identify it, it can then be deleted out of their vibrational path and they will never have to live with disease, disharmony, conflict, or anything that is not favorable. Humans can learn to eliminate wars, murder, and all forms of violence by changing their vibrational force to extend the light that they are.

"There is an actual blueprint that your species carries in its DNA of their original, beautiful ethereal paradigm before the fall of man into the physical. This knowledge is awakening now for the rebuilding of a peaceful light and love frequency on the Earth. It is awakened by spreading this vibration whether by one on one, in groups or in multitudes. It will eventually spread from nation to nation and then throughout the entire planet. Together, we can pull these transforming light waves together to evolve into the fourth- and fifth-dimensional paradigms. The universal forces do work, and assistance is always available. Julius is one of our highest beings in charge of emotional vibrational tones and balance. He is available to step in and answer any question humans may have on this subject. However, remember, humans are on a third-dimensional level and the high technical science of our methods may not be comprehended.

"It is important that emotions continue to be experienced on your planet because of the construct from which humans operate. However, it is paramount to learn how to control them, so as not to negatively affect the other parts of yourselves and the environment, as they presently do. The key word here is to detach and make wiser decisions based on rational thought or intuition rather than primarily a feeling state."

"The Blue Crystal beings, on the other hand, do not feel the negative emotions because we do not deal with negativity on our planet. We do deal with imperfections or things that may get in the way of progress as we see it, but when emotions do come up, we have the ability to instantly change them, and get a clear read-out of why we do become disconnected from the light. Usually we get separated for only a few moments or in small increments. We also have a support system that sheds new light on the matter so that we come to a better understanding of the condition of the being involved or the cause of the separation.

"Now, when we experience positive charges or emotions such as joy, happiness, ecstasy, or even humility, we can magnify that feeling hundreds of times, so it is felt throughout our land, and those around us are given a boost of magnificent light, love and support. It takes a great deal of effort and energy for humankind to have this kind of feeling and to have it at all times, be it great or small. The closest we have come to observing it is when there is a group of people at a concert, show, or laughing at comedy, and they begin to experience a sense of oneness. However, even that does not come close to the positive emotions we produce on a planetary basis, for when the time or night is over and people go to their various homes, they lose that sense of unity quickly, and it diminishes. By contrast, we can maintain positive emotions in the light, and they expand and are not lost.

"We do come to your planet and try to put ourselves in your shoes so we can remember what it was like to experience the negative emotions. It is difficult for us, because we do not like to feel that way, and it is painfully foreign. It consumes our intrinsic nature at the time, and we can't wait to release it. When we do, we discharge it into the universe which deletes the negative vibrations. This is the way we observe and experience the emotions of your brothers and sisters. When we come back to our atmosphere or environment, we have to detox and rid ourselves of an outer layer that attaches to us while in your environment. It is like when earthlings engage in a toxic territory in their planet and have to wear outer clothing that is protective, and then, later scrub and clear out all the toxins. It is an analogy, but much more difficult for us to do. We can teach more about the process of detoxing and renewing."

As Darius was speaking, I was listening intently, and I interrupted him with a question. "Darius, can you explain how thinking on planet Earth became so distorted, destructive, and negative emotions developed? It seems as if we have drifted very far from our original perfected state, including our ability to control our thoughts and feelings."

He replied, "First of all, it is necessary to give you some background regarding your question. The Earth and its species are only a thumb print of all that exists in the Cosmos. The Earth is but a speck in the whole scheme of things, like a bubble that is transparent to all other universes, planets, and entities floating around in space in the higher dimensions.

"So 'they' can see humans, but humans cannot see 'them.' Now and then, humans do get glimpses of 'them' in spaceships, or on other planets within your telescopic views, or see shadows, ghosts, angels, guides, fairies and so on. But to the human naked eye, they are usually invisible. Some developed people are familiar with their third eye, which is located in the middle of the forehead, but enclosed for protection. This structure can be awakened and opened so that they have access to the other realms. Also, other dimensions can be accessed in dreams, when the physical form has temporarily been placed aside for rest, and travel takes place in the light bodies which are always a part of you.

"In the New Living Translation of the Bible in 1 Corinthians 13:12, it says, 'Now we see things imperfectly (see through a glass darkly), like puzzling reflections in a mirror, but then we will see everything with perfect clarity. All that I know now is partial and incomplete, but then I will know everything completely, just as God now knows me completely.' This text provides a statement for the condition mankind is in today and refers to the invisibility of the many beings in other realms. It alludes to the future when all this will be made clear and humans function in their light bodies most of the time.

"Now, let us refer to your question about the origination of the distorted-thinking process and negative emotions. When the planet was first created, Earth beings had their light bodies and had Heaven on Earth, for it was a replica of the Heavenly spheres. However, the species began to think that they were other than Heavenly and began to ingest part of the Tree of Life.

"This is the true Adam and Eve story written in your Bible. What that meant was that Adam and Even did not use their ethereal or light bodies, so they thought they had to eat literally to feed their physical bodies when, in fact, they did not have to sustain themselves this way. Then, as they began to function more and more from the physical level, they were 'lost' and could no longer live in their light bodies on the Earth plane, but had to learn how to use their physical bodies such as you have learn how to drive a car. This resulted in unhappiness and other dissatisfied feelings stemming from longing for their former higher state of being and the vast spiritual freedom they had lost. This contributed to the negative feelings you are asking about.

"Also, when in the light body or ethereal state, they did not have to literally think, but could magnetically transfer information and communication to one another in a telepathic way by the universal mind. With the fall back into the physical, they now had to learn how to survive and communicate in physical terms. They had to now utilize their soul minds to feed their physical brain a way to 'think' and a way of learning and communicating with each other.

"Now, the thinking apparatus evolved over time, as did the physical body. Because the light bodies did not operate in the same way as the physical, there was a gradual major adjustment. It's like putting a Volkswagen engine in a Cadillac. The energies that worked were not in sync, so there was constant shifting, and the process had to be slowed down or increased. The guides and Masters have been and are continuing to help in this process, so humans can evolve and remember their light bodies in order to better converse with other beings and dimensions. The goal is to raise human frequency to the fourth- and fifth-dimensional beings that they actually are, but not fully expressing.

"Encasing the brain in the physical body resulted in a lower type of density, which resulted in the requirement of increased physical effort to manage bodily functions, even though these were partially accomplished by the involuntary nervous system. Thinking and communicating were not meant to be so tedious because in the light body, they flow automatically. The human brain is simple and not as complex as we think. We can have the ability to graph every aspect and cellular structure, and pinpoint the many electrical circuits in the brain chemistry on a grid.

"Humankind's problem lies within the back, not the front part of the brain organ. It has to do with the electrical shortage or cut off from the lumbar area. It is a minor thing that can be adjusted. The current within that area just seems to slow down and not shut off, so it's a matter of speeding up the current to make the right timing of synapses, which is a simple procedure. There are many, many types of blood vessels that spark off and on, so they can't always catch the exact one that blows. This can and will be fixed. When an electrical current or shortage is not properly functioning, it affects the entire body complex and, particularly, the nervous system. This alone, can cause a malfunction in the motor area and the slowing down of the heart function. This can cause much fatigue in the body. The doctors have their understanding in reverse. The body can handle all functions of the vehicle itself, if the brain chemistry is working properly. However, we do clog up the arteries with fats, acid, and so on, but the brain chemistry or electrical and magnetic circuits can correct it. More attention should be paid to the body's electrical system than anything else.

"Communication should be similar to the hard drive in a computer, which is already set and programmed. In the present state of thinking on Earth, humans have to invent or imagine the program and work at it to manifest it in physical terms. Currently, they can automatically think things in their mind which then filters through the brain. Then, it is necessary to physically speak it or write it, so they can then read and decipher it in a way that they can understand the original thought.

"What if humans were able to just think in their mind and then transfer this information to one another without physically manifesting it? Would this not be much simpler? It is this way in their light bodies, for they can think in light waves. This can telepathically transfer to another Being so there would be no use in speaking or writing. This is the way things were perfected until humans decided to experiment on their own and built up the physical body that became a barrier to the way they communicated. The way they were originally perfected was to live and experience life in a much easier way by just thinking and creating in their minds the type of world they wanted to live in without the difficult manual way of manifesting things.

"The monks of long ago and even today who live high in the Himalayas can do this quite easily because they have not forgotten who they really are and where they came from. They are considered advanced beings because of this. They can even transport their physical bodies and be in two places at once. They remember that they are light bodies and are multitudinous souls.

"This is the process that we will try to teach humankind in their limited selves, so they can begin to use it effectively. Would it not be easier to be able to look at each other and receive a read out, as you do with a computer? Well, when the mind is stilled and there is a connection with the higher self, this will be done quite easily.

"Look at people such as Sylvia Brown, the famous psychic. All she does is literally tune in and work through light waves. She cuts to the chase in the sense that she does not have to go through the physical brain, but simply receives a readout of another being's condition. Of course, it would be even more efficient if she would look at the person and give the information telepathically without words, yet, she wants to share her ability and information so that the masses can understand and validate the information.

"So, now let's go back to the Bible. Is it not written that God created the Heavens and the Earth and the word was made flesh? How did God do this in seven days? It was accomplished through the advanced process of thinking, creating, and manifesting in the light wave format. We could give literally volumes of knowledge on the topic of thinking, however, we want to offer only practical information that humans will be able to use in their current frequency. There are many bubbles in the ability to comprehend this concept. Why bubbles? Because it is through these transparencies that we can help you change the way you think and how to think. The process must become pure in its beginning stages in order to eradicate these bubbles.

"Pure Thinking involves thinking and creating in light waves and holding only pure, positive vibrations can accomplish this. I will now give more information about how to think in light waves for this is an advanced process from where humans are now.

"Earthlings have the expression that an idea comes to them and a light bulb lights up. Well, thinking in light waves is exactly like this. It's like having the light bulb go off, only on a more consistent basis and then, information will be held for a long time until that idea is expressed or manifested.

"In order to do this, one quiets the mind and visualizes the sunlight filling his whole being. Then, using mind power, click on the bulb which is the way to signal the brain to turn on the light within his body. This is similar to turning on the ignition key in a car to get the engine started so it can operate and transport. The important idea here is that one must think with the mind, not the brain, to start up his engine in the physical body. Literally, one can transform the light into his whole being, and this adds other positive energies to the body system. This light comes in waves, so then tap into the waves or oscillating rhythms.

"Another analogy would be playing the piano or keyboard. One simply taps the right keys to manifest the music to his ears. If it is done properly, one hears beautiful music. However, when the wrong key is used, there is discord. It was meant for the humans to hear harmonious chords and to operate on a particular chord with a pleasing auditory result. However, since they have not learned or relearned to think in the light, they bring about much discord and a rambling of distortion and static.

"Once humans realign with the light, they will not have negative thinking and only the positive will shine through. Do you remember the song, 'This Little Light of Mine, I'm going to let it shine?' Well, this is what I mean. This is what the Christ taught from the beginning of His journey in the Earth plane. Some of the disciples got the message and tried to carry on the work. This is how Paul was able to write scripture some forty years after Christ died and resurrected. He wrote in the light which was imprinted in his cosmic mind when he was living with the Christ. So, you see, the light waves are eternal.

"Once again, we will teach mankind step by step how this process works. Sometimes they may have an idea or invention stored in their brain for a long time. Then, the light bulb goes off and they receive in useful steps:

"Step One: Clear the mind and quiet the physical body. Be still and know . . . listen.

"Step Two: Now, visualize the light or sunlight in your mind. Then, let it penetrate the entire body and reflect in every cell. You are now beginning to change cellular structure.

"Step Three: Now, begin to enter that light as if you are going right into the actual core of it. Use your ethereal body or light body to step into the light. It will feel as if you have put your dense material body to sleep and are imaging the ethereal body.

"Step Four: Now, bathe yourself in the light as if you are getting a full cleansing. Imagine that you are under a waterfall and are feeling the water caress your body and washing the old and replacing the new.

"Step Five: Now, allow your Cosmic or Soul Mind to take over. You will feel a type of ecstasy and warmth and love like no other. You are now embraced by the light!

"Step Six: You will not have to manually think but only receive the information given to you on any subject or topic that you choose.

"So, you can now allow this information to come through you effortlessly. It flows on a light wave and you are now able to receive.

"Step Seven: You can then bring this information down so it infiltrates through the Cosmic Soul Mind to the social Earth mind and thus, imprints into your brain so you can easily talk or write about it.

"Remember that there is much information available to you, and that by using this method you tap into the cosmic mind and are given access by the Godhead as was meant many eons ago. This is the technique that has enabled creative people such as artists, musicians, writers, and clairvoyants to receive ideas. They appear to be doing this automatically, but in fact are tapping in as I described. Each of you can do this, for this is the imprint and nature of living in the light that the Christ taught many centuries ago. Mankind has now begun to catch a glimpse of the light, and, yet, it has been available all along.

"Another explanation of how the light waves operate is that they are much like sound waves. Each person has his own blueprint of light or individual signature similar to their personal sound frequency. In order to achieve oneness and harmony within humanity, it's going to become necessary to bring each human into a blend of light that is harmonic. If you could see your light wave signature printed out on a computer it would look quite strange, but within your own soul you would recognize it. Once you can visualize your wave, you draw others into it by visualizing oneness with them and allowing your light to fuse with them in oneness.

"What happens is that the individual light waves oscillate at their own speed and begin to infuse and balance in accord so they act as one light, just as a choir sings in harmony and becomes one voice. For example, some of you sing lead, some baritone, some base and others tenor and still others in between. When you practice and come together you perform in harmony. Some of you say '. . . but I can't even sing on tune!' The answer is, 'Yes, you can.' The reason that you don't blend is because the sound waves that you came in or incarnated with are sounds that are yet to be found and heard by your ears. However, one day you will discover these other sound waves and will be amazed at the many melodious sounds within you.

"The same is true for blending the light of individual humans. Humans think they can't blend just like they think they can't sing harmony in a choir, however, some day they will discover within themselves the ability to call forth enough light to blend in oneness. Eventually, each point of light will infuse and become one with other points and this power will spread to all nations over the world. This is what is meant by 'So let your light shine.'"

In an instant, Darius was gently leading me back to my desk and I was conscious of typing at my computer. It had been a long session, but very uplifting and informative. I thanked him and with a loving touch, we parted in form only, as he was always with me and only a thought away.

I sat back in my chair and reflected in amazement on what I had learned. I felt alert and mentally and emotionally stimulated; however, it was just dawn, so I quietly returned to bed without waking Bert.

CHAPTER EIGHT

A Future Food for the Earth

*"My mind had a hard time with assimilation, but in my altered state
it was so effortless, and I could listen to their information forever,
and there were not time constraints."*

I woke up with a start after dozing somewhat peacefully. It was a bright
morning, and Bert was fixing breakfast in the kitchen. The aroma was
calling me, so I tossed the covers aside and got dressed as I normally did
and joined him at the kitchen table. He was smiling and patted the chair
and gave me a loving hug and kiss. I truly was blessed, and my heart
overflowed with my love for him. I could think of nothing else I would
rather do than be with him at this moment.

I mentioned briefly some of the information on emotions and thinking that I had received the night before. He was only too aware of the
need for a more constructive use of emotions and the thinking process
on the Earth plane, so I did not think it necessary to go into detail. He
was fascinated with the ability of the Blue Crystal beings to simply clear
out negative emotions instantly.

After work that day, I chose to relax and rest and assimilate all the information I had received. I felt a constant presence of the beings, while in my counseling office, but especially when I just rested. It was as if they were attending to my needs on all levels and restoring me for our next encounter.

That night, I eagerly went to my computer with an urgency to write. I had a feeling of oneness and more connectedness as I continued with these beings. It was such pleasure to work with them that I can't express it in words. My mind had a hard time with assimilation, but in my altered state it was so effortless. I could listen to their information forever and there were no time constraints. This is difficult to explain, but I will just accept what and how this information was given to me. I feel blessed for this opportunity. After loving greetings from my Blue Crystal guides, I was invited to take another tour.

Several guides were assigned to me, and as we approached the outer environment of the Blue Crystal Planet, I did not see rivers, lakes or oceans as such, but instead reflective pools of a water-like material that I cannot easily describe, somewhat in the form of rivers, lakes and oceans. Later in this journey, I had the opportunity to place my hand in this substance, and it consisted of cooling and undulating pulsating sensations and was so smooth to the touch, as if one were touching clouds or soft cotton balls. It was unlike anything I had ever seen or felt in my life on Earth.

As we traveled, my guide tried to explain, "You could swim in this substance, or rather float on waves, but much differently than the way you are floating or moving about in what you would call our atmosphere. There are pathways or routes in these reflective oceans and lakes that can carry one on long distances at a relatively short period of what you would call time. We do have a different navigating system, but it is too difficult to explain in your terms."

What I especially noticed is that they could travel at extremely high speeds or at speeds that looked as if they were standing still. In other words, it would look like they were not moving, and they could take in the view of other places or areas on their planet simultaneously at their leisure as they were moving, so as to arrive at another destination. It would be like us in a ship stopping at various ports or places of interest without losing traveling time. What a concept!

Next, they accelerated my rate of speed to a place that I would call another city, but for them it was only a gathering place or point of interest where other projects were being worked on. This was a "city" that glowed green and when you looked through it, there were many hues of green. I was amazed.

The guide stated, "This is a place where groups are gathered to study a replica of the Earth's environment and its nature world. They work individually or in groups in a highly motivated and harmonious way. We are experimenting with a new form of vegetation for consumption on the Earth. It is a type of food product that will be introduced to your environment in the near future. We cannot consume it, but we can manipulate it to change its structure so we get an idea of what it might taste like and how it can be digested in the human body. We can then change it to adapt to the Earth beings. We do not grow it in soil, but use a liquid-like substance that has all the nutrients needed for the physical body to be sustained."

It was unlike anything I had ever seen, but it did resemble our vegetation, only the colors were more bright and light. They told me that it had a higher frequency than the foods we currently ate and that by consuming this product, it will have all the nourishment humans need without the supplements you take and it will energize you, as well as give feelings of wellness and create a type of calming in our system. It will also reorganize your immune system so you would not have as much vulnerability to disease. This new food system will be what you call a miracle food and it will sustain you for longer periods of time. It will also regulate our metabolism so we would not have to worry about weight problems, and all of the human species would operate at optimum levels. This will be introduced by the year 2020 in small increments. There are Earth scientists and agriculturists that are working on this in small ways presently. The idea will be infused into the minds of your species who are working in the scientific fields to improve your food chains. They have the ability to infuse this information in the altered or sleep state of various individuals on Earth who are dedicated to improve the health and wellness of both the physical and mental minds and bodies of your species. I was told to be looking for this in the near future. This new food, of course, would be grown organically as we work with purifying the Earth soil and environment and later, the idea of growing this vegetation in a new liquid format will come about.

My guide informed me that in 50 years or so, or even sooner, our species will begin to look strikingly different, much slimmer, lighter, with different body colors or hues and the auras will take on a new dimension.

There were literally thousands and thousands of acres of these food types grown here, and I could not see the end; it was so vast. They told me that they created this product for man's consumption here in a purified environment first, so they could bring about the purified energies or rather non-contaminated energies that work together. They had to develop the life force that could sustain it before they entered it into our environment. There were many modifications, adjustments, and re-adjustments that had to take place. In other words, this had to be perfected on their planet, first, before it could be transported to another planet such as ours.

I asked, "Why do you do this and not have our own species develop this new, healthy vegetation?"

"It's because of our advanced knowledge, wisdom and mission to bring about this product in order to speed up the food system before it is too late. Humans are contaminating their food chain and products and by consuming these, are literally poisoning themselves. Our mission is to assist the Earth in these kinds of advancements in order to save the planet and themselves, as a species, from destruction. The Earth is in an especially slow, evolving paradigm and it would take eons of time to reach the growth that we are assisting the planet to achieve, and your linear time space environment will not be able to wait or catch up.

"An analogy would be that you saw a child crossing the street with a vehicle coming at him at high speed and you could not outrun it to grab the child to save him. However, should a high frequency entity or an angel guide appear who had the ability to quickly snatch up the child before that car hits him, then the child would be saved and safe from any harm. We are here to assist mankind to hasten the safe-guards and to protect them from harm in any way. This is a simplified version of what we do, but it will suffice for now. We are working in the best interest of humankind as well as in our best interest to serve, do you understand?"

I replied, "Yes, I do know there is so much you do that we cannot begin to comprehend. I am just overwhelmed with all I am learning. It is difficult for me to grasp the immense energy exertion your beings engage in for our planet, yet, I can begin to sense it when I come here. It just overwhelms me!"

My guide continued, "Yes, I understand. Now, the green area you are presently visiting is all about this particular food project. It is a joy to behold because each time we invent a better product to help the Earth, we celebrate with songs, and music and dancing with the heavenly spheres, as we are a community of love and compassion. This work also is connected with the increased opening of the human DNA double helix and the more these are activated, the more advanced humankind will become."

Directing me he said, "Come with me now, and I will show you our tasting area."

I was taken to a place of a particular green hue that was comical to observe. They were actually testing the new food products on themselves to see how we would like it. However, when they tried to taste it, they could not remain in their light bodies and were required to alter their molecular structure to be close to ours. I saw them making all kinds of faces and distortions with their bodies and it was a sight to see.

When the product was more perfect, they were so excited and exhilarated, almost like what we would call in a drunken state. In their altered lowered frequency vibration they looked a little like humans, but in a different way that is hard to explain. They, of course, did not like to be in this state for long, so they worked to change and modify the energies back to their usual frequencies rather quickly. To be in their altered state even for short periods had the same effect on them as humans would experience if drunk for an extended period of time. The being explained that they were careful while experimenting, so they had their protective guides always present who can manipulate the energies to bring them back to their natural state.

The beings began bidding me a safe journey back home, so I knew I was soon to be departing. Again, I was zoomed back to Earth and was conscious of typing at my computer. Bert was standing in the doorway gazing at me with concern and love, and helped me in my sleepy state to find my way to bed.

CHAPTER NINE

A Day in the Life of a Blue Crystal Being

*"They also explained that when they observe humans in their altered states
of being such as during resting or sleeping, we resemble them and are able
to do things that we cannot do while in our physical bodies."*

It was 5:30 in the morning on a Sunday. I woke up and could not sleep and, again, had the urgency to write. It's strange how the guides work, or probably more strange how our brains work. It is as if sometimes our channels are wide open and other times quite closed. I guess it is like a radio or television in that when reception is good there are no problems, while at other times channels are hazy and there is static. So it is with being open and clear minded, for when we expand our receptors, information is given and the channels are clear. The information flows in such a more understanding way, and one can write, and the words just cascade. Such was my state, as I relaxed into my computer chair.

Darius stood beside me glowing in immense, golden energy and light, an expectant smile on his elegant, handsome face. As I allowed myself to drift into a trance state, he clarified how difficult it was for Blue Crystal beings to communicate their high frequency information so it can be received by an Earth being.

He explained, "It is most difficult for us to bring information in this way and to impress your brain with our frequencies, so that we can put it into words and mankind can understand as they receive it. Think how difficult it would be to speak to a first grader in college language. Multiply that a thousand times or more and then you can understand to a small degree how difficult it is for us to communicate in our language so mankind receives our messages.

"I must say that we do have more patience than Earthlings, for we have eternity here and there are no limits or time constrictions. The only limits are that there are opportune moments or intervals in your time frame for information to be shared and knowledge to be dispensed, so that it fits into the whole scheme of things."

I knew he was referring to how important it was to get this book published and available to the people on Earth and I nodded in agreement as I took his outreached hand to drift slowly towards the Blue Crystal Planet.

He continued: "Today, I would like for you to discover what it is like to experience a day in the life of your cosmic brother or sister on our majestic Blue Crystal Planet. Since we do not operate here in a time constraint, we will give you a simulation of what a typical day would be like. Remember that there are many types of beings here on multiple levels working on various planet and space projects, so we will pick one level and go from there. You will also become acquainted with the nature of the animal life which is a little different than yours on Earth."

They now took me to what I would consider the outdoors. There was no in or out or direction as in our environment, or coded in our brains and five senses. As I floated outward it was so vast that I felt like I was traversing the universe and the strange thing was that I did not see sky or clouds or stars, only a kind of limitless space. They had to alter my brain to be able to encompass it, or take it all in. Then, I felt more comfortable and could catch glimpses of space. I looked about and floated downward sort of, and saw the beautiful landscape they had created.

I saw what appeared to be a replica of our Earth wildlife jungles with similar colors. This was so impressive, that I felt just like I was at home! There were trees, forests, brush, mountains, and lakes similar to Earth only much more immense and luscious in detail. Here, it was just vast and open, and, when I looked up, there appeared to be sky or a colorful umbrella over this delightful jungle.

As I gently floated over this vibrant, iridescent, green area spreading out below me, I desired to sink into the inviting branches reaching out to me. I breathed in fragrances which were refreshingly earthy and pungent, and I was amazed to find myself in the middle of a many intriguing grasslands, meadows, and trees which seemed to be extend infinitely into the horizon.

I saw ahead of me huge fields of flowers of all kinds and colors and so many different fragrances. I could stay there for eons and the guides told me that this is what happens when you cross over and decide to incarnate into their planet. They also explained that when they observe humans in their altered states of being, such as during resting or sleeping, we resemble them and are able to do things that we cannot do while in our physical bodies. It's only in our physical state that we have such struggles and get stuck in our solidity. They said we actually spend more time in our light bodies than our physical, but we do not at this time have the ability to change our molecular structure while in a conscious state of mind, and have the abilities that they have. In time, we will be able to do this and, then, to shed our physical vehicles and maintain our light bodies as they do.

As I took all of this in, I noticed that the atmosphere did not feel hot or cold to me. I was comfortable and did not need any kind of clothing or gear there. My light ethereal body was adapting well and I did not feel temperature. Also, they said it did not rain, for there was no need for it. Then, they told me that what we call space or vastness on their planet did have levels. As we experienced this, we would feel an energy change, movement or a type of vacillation. Their bodies adjust well to this, but humans have to have theirs worked on, so we have their assistance all the time in energy adjustments when we travel outside our physical bodies. They have a method or are coded to automatically change frequency when this happens. It would be like us in our own atmosphere traveling up to the stratosphere.

It was so much to behold! I felt as if I was in heaven, and, yet, they said this is only one of the heavenly realms. They said their purpose was to assist the Earth planet, and in order to do this, their planet had to realign itself close to the Earth's planetary axis and level of evolution on its parallel orbit. This is why it was called our sister planet, and, as they explained this, I felt such a harmonious connection and affection for these beings and their habitation.

I saw grass, bushes, trees and flowers unlike any that I would recognize, for these things pulsated with energy composed of light atoms and were very much alive. It was as if I could see inside each leaf or petal, and it had so much life to it that I felt compelled to honor it. They reached out to me and were as fascinated with me as I was with them. It was truly incredible! The guides were laughing, for I was like a baby on Earth seeing for the first time and putting things in my mouth to taste to get a sense of what it was.

The fragrances were so prominent that they infused my being, so I smelled with all the cells of my body. This was especially true when I inhaled the intoxicating aroma of a rose. What an experience! Everything there was of a higher frequency and so beyond description that I could hardly take it all in. It was like being in a museum and spending days upon days and still not experiencing everything, only here it was in moments. I guess this is what was meant by eternity or timelessness. They explained that they have a fragrance that is so atomic that it was actually absorbed in their bodies and was quite healing to their very souls. They said if we could absorb these they would rid our Earth of the bad bacteria and viruses of our planet. They compared it to our aromatherapy, which was a blueprint of their fragrances, however, we, in our present state cannot replicate theirs. The energy would be overwhelming and humans would be unable to absorb it in the way that they do. They reminded me that we are in parallel universes with them and that is why the fragrances were similar on Earth, but of a much lower frequency, and that it will take many more years for the Earth to catch up.

As I gazed about, I noticed that I did not see any type of insects, for the plants do not require pollination as they do on Earth. They are created by like cosmic minds and thoughts that are held together for whatever time or interval needed. The plants do not die nor do they need nourishment like vegetation on Earth. They are sustained through thoughts of the beings who care for them. They also have a kind of communication, in that they speak or vibrate messages to those who care to receive. They are amazing creations unto themselves.

They let me lower my frequency so I could actually feel the meadows and fields around me. It felt like I was, again, sinking into it and that it became a part of me. There was nothing separate there, for everything was bound together with everything else. No one felt alone here, not even the nature types of beings. They are always surrounded by light, harmony, and love, so much so, that one does not want to leave this place ever. This was the heaven on Earth that God spoke about and the beings here were working so close with the Earth to gradually bring about this type of environment. We have a long way to go, but I know that we, too, someday will evolve to this marvelous state of being.

As I drifted down a bit, I observed various types of animal creatures. They did not look as dense as ours and they appeared less beastly and their bodies radiated rainbow hues of colors with a type of fur that I was told was unusually soft to the touch. They were tame and sort of grazed with each other and the grass they consumed appeared to remain alive within their bodies. The actual blades of grass sustained their own individual existence while in the animals and gave them nourishment, and that was quite different! When complete, the blades were then released into another form to grow and develop. It was an astonishing sight to see! I could actually view the grass giving nourishment to the animal's transparent body. They first appeared to be solid, but then as I looked again, I noticed that because they were in a light body form, one seemed to be superimposed on the other.

These animals were remarkably exotic, and had total freedom to roam the area. It is difficult to describe them for at first you might see what could be a dog, but with different features, or a lion, tiger, horse, cat, or zebra, sort of like replicas of the Earth counterpart, but of different coloration, and made of different material.

The creatures here emitted quite unusual sounds. For example, a dog did not bark, but gave out sounds sort of in a sing song, musical fashion. It was not harsh to the ears, but was a melodic type of vibration. That was the case with the other creatures. The bird-like ones did not actually have wings like ours, but were imbued with bands or strands of energy in various tones and frequencies which allowed them to sort of float above the other animals. They had such a sweet, lilting intonation, much more serene and peaceful than the birds on Earth. I longed to stay here for a long time and relax among them. They were quite tame and friendly and liked to play and frolic.

When I floated to the ground, they drew near and observed me, for I was of a different world and they could sense that. However, they gave off energy of such unusual love and emotion, that I felt no fear, and knew I was unconditionally accepted by them. I even stroked their sort of fur or feathers which, of course, had quite strange sensations compared to Earth animals. They were so affectionate that it was difficult to leave them and I wanted to spend more time. It was explained to me that these creatures are revered, for they play a part, like devas on the Earth, in the growth and well-being of plants and other life forms.

These beings were well taken care of by their caretakers, who also had ethereal forms as well, with a more distinct human shape with lots of greens and blue hues exuding from them. They were so gentle, not only among themselves, but with the creatures. The task of these caregivers was to teach the animals how to interact with their species and to assist them to interact with the animal creatures on Earth. Their job was to bring a higher consciousness to the Earth animal kingdom and to somewhat tame them. One day they, too, will be docile and not harm humans or other animals. This is going to take time, but animal consciousness on the Blue Crystal Planet can help animal consciousness on Earth. This may be a hard concept to understand. These beautiful creatures can communicate with each other as well as with the Blue Crystal beings. You see, there is a universal language among all mankind and planetary beings as well as among the animal kingdom.

Darius explained, "As a human you have a desire to understand your animals' language, and one day you will. For now, you have to use your intuitive senses and can sort of communicate, in a way, on a psychic level. However, your dog, for instance, can understand another dog's language, and they bark and converse together. You notice that they bark in unison which means that they can telepathically speak on another level to each other. If you listened intently, you could distinguish levels of intonation and communicate when a dog is hungry, thirsty, angry, irritated or agitated, or even when he senses harm or hears an intruder. These are forms of communication, and a more evolved understanding will be common in the future."

The guides then told me that I could come back and observe and play more later, for it was time for me to enter another arena. With great difficulty, I allowed myself to be steered in a different direction.

Darius declared, "Let's visit an area that is similar to the Earth in a way, and simpler and less complex. Your guides and I would like to begin with the Crystal Academy. Now, remember that this is not a village or neighborhood like yours, but a place of various crystals put together in a unique pattern for diverse intended functions. Each Being enters at his or her level. It would be like various schools of study within your colleges.

"I will work diligently with you and allow you to have this experience from your vantage point. However, would you be willing to lie down and let us simulate one of our days without your cumbersome typing, so you can actually experience the mental and emotional level? Perhaps later an assistant could conduct you in a trance state or hypnotic state of mind. But for now, allow us to take you in your higher mind to this amazing place."

I nodded my consent to his request and was quite familiar with having a conductor guide me in trance sessions. However, for the moment I found traveling in my higher mind quite pleasant.

As I was zoomed up, I was departing from the beautiful Earth at a rather rapid pace in a whirl of white and blue energy. Everything was magically swirling in an array of colors, and I was going farther and farther out, leaving behind everything that was familiar and felt like home. It was like leaving your parents to go to college, only much more intense. As I distinguished the lustrous lights of other planets in space, I did not detect the usual upward feeling, but instead felt a sensation similar to traveling across the United States in a straight line from the East coast to the West coast. Darius and my guides accompanied me and were my constant navigators, and no explanation was offered as to this change in my sense of direction.

As we were traveling, they commented that when we crossed over and left our physical bodies behind permanently as in so-called death, many of our guides and spiritual teachers rescued and guided us to reach our various destinations in the spiritual realms. It then took time, or intervals, to learn to direct ourselves on our own. This is the way our soul or light bodies learn to project either back to our Earthly home or to other planets or dimensions after passing over to the Other Side.

By now, being quite comfortable in my light body, I easily looked down at myself, and was in awe of me, this magnificent radiant spirit created by our God. I was a transparent, iridescent Being so beautiful in an array of colors and light. This was my ethereal body, and I could escape the third-dimensional form from time to time, as I was doing at this moment. I did not care if I returned to my physical body, for this was heaven to me. But they told me that I would be given instruction to return when I have had my experience with them, for it was not my time to lay my physical body down or die.

I began swirling into a brilliant vortex and was encompassed and embraced in so much light and love. These beings here were truly accepting, and I did not have to prove myself, just be myself, unlike entering our colleges or higher learning places on Earth where we somehow have to try to make ourselves fit in or be accepted. Here, I was automatically accepted, and I recognized the feeling of unconditional love. I was gracefully and carefully rotated downward into a most beautiful, colorful place called the Crystal Academy which was one of the most striking areas I had ever visited. Yet, a part of me sensed a familiarity there as it emanated the energy of my cosmic home. I did not fear anything, for I was surrounded with much love from my space sisters and brothers.

Darius explained that they did have a kind of level or attainment in this Academy, but did not use terms like freshman or sophomore. They were just where they were, and no one here thought the less of it, or judged their achievement. Everyone was most willing for me to understand their learning process, and there were many teachers to show me the way.

I gazed with my ethereal eyes at a delightful entrance of translucent crystal that reflected green and blue gradations, kind of like a crystallized teal, but entirely more striking. Clearly indescribable, I felt as if I were entering blue-green water similar in nature to the glassy, clear waters of Hawaii on the Earth. As I entered this phase of the Academy, these undulations of energy were soothing and healing, as if they blessed the soul. I encountered a cleansing sensation, like water, only I did not perceive any texture to the colors, but, instead, felt inward waves of another essence unlike waves of water. It consumed my entire ethereal being with such contentment that I felt like I always wanted to return to this place. It was so overwhelming that I believed that I could live out eternity here. Next, I was guided into an endless space and was taken to a portion of it. There were no individual rooms, as in our academies, only space as far as the eye could see. They had to direct me to the area where I needed to be at that moment. I sensed that an encompassing essence was closing in around us, yet I did not have the perception that I was in a room. It was a strange, peculiar sensation to be enclosed like this, and not discern walls.

As I began to gaze around with my ethereal eyes, I recognized other beings here similar to those I had seen in other visits to the Blue Crystal Planet. I was included as a member of an amazing group of students who were accommodating their teaching modality just for me. I had to learn to adjust my vibration to be able to access the information with my light body and cosmic mind. It did take a while, like on Earth as if putting on a scuba diving suit to acclimate to the water. After a brief adjustment, there I was, feeling so highly motivated to learn that I could hardly wait to get on with it, unlike classes in colleges, where I could hardly wait till the class was over, and had difficulty returning to the next session. What a feeling it was! Information was delivered on a screen in a holographic style; it was visual, but also I felt it enter my body in a tingling, invigorating sensation. It was highly motivating, but in a much different, creative presentation that appealed to all our senses. Everyone there was catching on, yet it was a kind of group learning. They expressed such happiness and joy that I was there, and I savored so much this special connectedness, as if we were sharing the same emotions as one being.

So, I learned in this experience what it was like to participate in a school day with them, and being included in their learning process. The time there seemed like eternity to me, and I learned much about these beings; it was incredible. When the visitation at the Academy was complete, it was not like an end, but more like a beginning, for I desired to continue more and more. I did not feel tired or hungry, but in a way there was still a remembrance of my Earthly body and I did feel the need to rest and nourish myself. They took quite good care of me. I asked them where they go after the day at school is complete. They laughed as if it was a dumb question, because they do not live within time or days in their reality, but they promised to show me where they go after school which they said was a kind of home.

Darius zoomed in front of me with a burst of excitement, "Wait, before you experience our homes, I want to explain how differently we manifest our dwellings. You see, it's hardly comparable to how humans build their housing on the Earth. Humans must work with a great deal of effort to build their homes from already solid materials. First, you choose the right location, then the right contractors, then the materials and work out a blueprint form in which you choose the design that you desire. It is interesting to us to watch mankind choose where they will reside their physical bodies. It is an arduous task, and it takes a lot a time and energy to do so. What is different for us on the Blue Crystal Planet is that there exists no such space or location upon which to create an abode. We must create it by simply tuning into the necessary vibration and frequency level adaptable to our family, or our group family.

"We do not feel the need to separate ourselves like you, nor do we feel the compulsion for privacy, for we are always exposed to one another, but in a much different way. We do not need this like you do, but from time to time we do recognize our family members and do live or reside together. Sometimes this is for the purpose of revisiting past experiences just for fun, like on Earth, when you look at old videos of family events.

"When we decide that we want to create a place to dwell from the past either with our heavenly family or soul family, we counsel with other guides that are knowledgeable about creating the correct grids and energy patterns that bring about the manifestation of the blueprint we have all agreed upon. Then, we map it out in our cosmic minds, and begin the process of building form, which, of course, is not solid or physical like yours, but on an ethereal level. We would view it like a solid as would you, but in actuality, it is of a type of metallic magnetic energy form with a type of membrane that holds it together. It has to be created according to the crystal-power formula and maintained as such.

"The shape our buildings take can be modeled after our memory of lives we once lived on Earth or other types of structures as seen or visited on other planets. They can be formed like architectural designs that you have on Earth—what you call Contemporary, Modern, Log house, Colonial, Victorian, Pioneer, Farm house, European, English Tudor, and so on. We would just go back to the memory of that which we had experienced, and recreate it. It could be spacious or small dimensions, whatever the family agrees upon. However, we would not need doors to enter or windows, but there would be a facade of a door as such, and we would be able to walk through it or float through or above or below to enter. The house would provide a contained space for the moment, so we can recollect and pull our memories together.

"We create a type of furniture upon which to recline, and we meditate or watch a screen that depicts Earth life as it once was. It is like going down Memory Lane and we do cherish this, as there are times in which we really miss the physical way of living. We gather together and then create a type of food similar to yours and ingest it into a type of made-up body, since we do not have physical bodies. This way we can get a taste of your food, and then we simply get rid of it through the ethers and it dissipates. We nourish ourselves through re-energizing, and our energy levels change in accordance. We enjoy these simulations of other expressions of life, and we do this from time to time. It is like an astronaut who wishes to experience a trip to space and simulates it with many, many trials of practice and, likewise, we do this when we wish to simulate other forms, such as Earth life.

"Remember, in our reality we are always given crystal energy and light, and this is how our light bodies function. If you wanted to replicate our life style, and if you were able to, this is how it might work. You would first put yourselves in a clear and gravity-free environment like your astronauts and simply float about. Then, you would have to learn how to navigate your bodies so you would be able to land where you wish and hold in place your light bodies.

"Next, you would begin to learn that you do not need the type of foods grown on Earth, but a new type of nourishment that is energized with the proper nutrients and elements that sustain the light body. After that, you would have to tune into your ethereal bodies and view yourselves much as we see ourselves as higher fourth- or fifth-dimensional beings. You would realize that your mode of communication would be vastly different because you would not have to use touch, taste, sight, or audible sounds. You couldn't even try to eat, for you would not have a mouth designed for that. You would simply see yourself as your own magnetic energized body or vehicle, and you would tune into the necessary dials that would transmit the energy needed to sustain you. You would feel so ecstatic that it is unimaginable to the human mind.

"You would not feel tired, or the need to sleep, so you would begin to explore days, weeks, month, and years in your time in just a matter of moments. Like a flash, things come to you in moments. It can be highly overwhelming, so we send you guides to help you with this process. It is a WOW experience that you can bring back with you and store in your memory banks as a reserve for you to use the rest of your Earthly life. Isn't that incredible? You would not have the need to sleep, but you would have the need to rest, for you are being transformed into a light entity which will require moments to rest the mind body and soul. You would recline your fifth-dimensional light body on a type of furniture that we have designed for that purpose, but it will actually feel as if you are riding a cloud in a substance so soft and porous, that it actually relaxes your entire being unlike anything you have ever experienced before.

"When it's time for you to complete your restful state, you will come to or wake up so refreshed and revitalized, that you feel like you can hold this feeling for eternity. You really can, but then you begin to realize it has been a dream and you must come back to your Earthly reality. What a shame, for this is the state that you mostly reside in when you begin to remember who you really are. When it is time to return to your Earthly destination, you feel a kind of separation and dullness, and then you are whipped or jolted back into your physical body. You may wonder where you have been for some time, but your guides will help you to again readjust and to begin to remember bit by bit. So this is how you would simulate living as a light body and the Blue Crystal beings will continue to help Earthlings evolve toward this goal."

I reclined in relaxing manner, while Darius explained all this to me. I was curious as to what type of home I would be invited to, but I soon found out. Thanking Darius for such stimulating information, I stretched my arms toward my guides who were patiently waiting for me to respond to their beckoning.

I was taken outwards, and I literally zoomed out of the teal crystal college and found myself viewing a series of odd-shaped dwellings that only slightly resembled a home on Earth. I looked around and saw quite unusual abodes that were crystallized with utter, clear beauty and light and luminous, unearthly colors. They were iridescent with various hues of blue, violet, white and gold. Their houses varied from one to another, depending on the type in accordance with each person, family, and group. They liked to be among their own kind with similar frequencies, which made it a supportive and harmonious environment. Their dwelling places did not lie in rows or neighborhoods like ours, but in patterns unlike I had ever seen. They were constructed of various crystals put together, some close, others on bottom and still others on top. It was very distinctive, and quite attractive. They could enter their dwellings from the top, sideways, or any direction. They simply distinguished the correct frequency and code to enter.

I was in a gathering place of astounding beings exuding much love and acceptance. Each one wanted to take me to their home, so, as a group they decided together where that would be. They explained that there would be warmth and nourishment, but unlike our physical experiences on Earth.

Next, I felt a feminine energy being escorting me toward her dwelling. I was navigating in what seemed to be a western direction, although there were no directions there. She explained that they needed a type of rest period to recharge their light bodies, and they used a dwelling place for this purpose. I was brought to lovely pinkish, glowing dome, and I felt instant acceptance by the other beings present as they reached out to envelope me in their blazing light. When I entered, I had the feeling of total love and relaxation, even though I did not lie down or sit down and relax my light body. The beings and I floated, stood, or reclined in whatever position resulted in renewing of ourselves. Inside was enormous space, but some of it was void or empty and some was filled to the brim with other beings as well. They did not have obstacles to get in the way and they did not get in the way of each other, for they had the ability to pass through things because the density was not as solid as it would be on Earth. I soon settled myself in a lovely, soft, comfortable area resplendent with soothing colors, mainly hues of pink.

I began to hear a stirring sound like a million musicians playing classical music, and it appeared as if an actual orchestra and singers were right there before my eyes and ears. It was such a harmonious performance, so soothing beyond the frequencies of Earth, and totally sublime. Also, there was a heavenly fragrance of innumerable roses or some other flowers surrounding me, which resembled being out in nature on the Earth, and I did not have to leave the dwelling to experience this unless I wanted to. There was celestial energy all around me, and I wanted to stay there and bathe in all of this, for my ethereal body needed to adjust. Since there was no concept of time, we rested and recharged quite rapidly. In each home there was a type of revitalizing machine like a giant electric magnetic device that they gathered or floated around. Various colors of light waves entered their bodies and emitted a special sound when they completed the re-energizing process. I was told I could not recharge with this machine or I would be blown away—not my soul, of course, but my light body, which would then be automatically sent back to Earth to my physical body. Of course, I had no desire to leave, and I only hoped the feeling I experienced in this dwelling would stay with me permanently.

I was taken on a tour through the rest of this abode and again, there was no separation of rooms, but mostly undefined chambers. They did not have bedrooms, as such, but a type of lounging, soft area where they rested their light bodies and sunk into a type of furniture made of materials I had never seen and which looked like billowy clouds. They just drifted into it and sort of reclined and enjoyed the state of being where they recreated or went into a type of dream state and brought to their attention anything they wanted to contemplate such as past lives on Earth or other dimensions, planets and stars. They had the ability to be in the present moment and the future all at the same instant. One of the beings let me see what he was thinking in pictures so he could bring it down to my perception. He told me that, in time, we will accelerate to do this as well.

Next, I was taken to an area that I would call the kitchen, but it was much more. They did not need nourishment such as we do for our physical bodies, but partook of a kind of substance that gave sustenance to their light bodies. I was consumed with delightful smells that I had never experienced. Their cooking did not involve animals or plant life or vegetables. It was a type of food that they could utilize in the electrical disposition of their light bodies. It provided energy and a form of nutrient which they consumed which stimulated their technical systems with the correct adjustments for their vehicle.

They went to various areas of the kitchen and put together potions like you would see in a lab, and mixed these up and poured them into a type of orifice within their own bodies. This included a system of dials which they manipulated. They had the exact amount down to a science and did not have to excrete for their bodies used and stored these types of ingredients. They usually had to do this nurturing only once a week in our time. They did employ various gases and liquids to lubricate their systems and to add the necessary ingredients to sustain them for long periods of time. These discharged a fragrance and type of taste, but not as we would know it.

For myself, my guide mixed a potion of liquid like a milkshake and upon drinking it, I felt it being absorbed in my ethereal body similar to feeding my physical body. They said it was important for me to remember that I was of the human species and required a different type of nutrient than they did. The milkshake smelled like a beautiful garden of gardenias and was strawberry flavored, so it went down well. Afterward, I felt as if I did not have to eat or feed my body for a long time. I had energy and a sense of wellness and was quite refreshed. When I remarked that I wanted to take this feeling of wellness back with me, they said I could and would program it into my physical brain before I returned to Earth.

Next, they took me to a living area where several entities were gathered around. They were reclining on various types of chairs, but I cannot describe the material, but the colors were magnificent and they appeared to be seamless and were not separate units, and one flowed into the other without invading each other's space. They were discussing matters concerning their daily activities as well as their current projects. They had a kind of sense of humor and when they laughed, it came out like a type of indescribable squealing sound. It was of such a high pitch and they all squealed or laughed together somewhat as we do on Earth. I observed that I could actually see the waves of energy come out of them in colors of bright red, green, yellow and more. There was a unique oneness present, no conflict or animosity, only differing ideas which were happily accepted by all.

I asked one of the males about what their family units were like. He said that families sometimes were of a basic group of beings that repeatedly remained together, but mostly groups of beings came together on a daily basis for support of their interests or projects, not based on a relationship or birth history or previous times together. However, they did replicate or rebirth new souls into their group. This was based on different levels of spiritual development, and not phases of growth as we have here going from infants to adulthood to seniors.

I asked about R and R and he said they had a kind of recreation in which they did engage. This included various games that they created and recreated such as materializing a type of ball or sphere that they spun around. They had mind games or video games that they made up as they went along and tried to stump each other. It was fun to watch, however, they were not competitive like us, and did not have to win. They only did this to exercise their brain power, but it clearly demonstrated their usage of abilities of thinking and interacting that was far beyond the Earth, and more cosmic in nature. They did not have spectator sports as we do, for they did not feel they needed to entertain others in this fashion.

Darius allowed me to rest in this lovely home for a period of time. As I relaxed in this immense beauty and peace, I thought about the beings I had visited earlier who used a revitalizing machine to recover and renew themselves and how I was not allowed to use it.

This led me to recall an experience several years earlier on Earth when I was awakened in the middle of the night when Bert and I were sleeping. Several beams of bright, dazzling light in the shape of a rectangular, highly technical machine hovered over Bert as he lay sleeping. I could not believe my eyes! It was so amazing to me because it was unlike anything I had ever seen on the Earth. I did not know where it came from, but telepathically it was revealed to me that these beams of light radiated over his body to deliver cosmic energy into his soul being. Their purpose was to sustain his life force in doing the higher work in service to others as was planned in his soul contract for this lifetime. I always wondered where he received so much energy and why he did not need to sleep for long periods of time as do most humans. The colors glowing from the machine were magnificent with bright reds, greens, purple, blues, yellow, golden, white and other hues that I did not recognize. I also was told that the colors held various frequencies and patterns, unlike those of Earth. They were filled with a love vibration that I had never experienced before. Bert was asleep through this whole process, but I knew that on some level he was being nourished through this heavenly, Godly power. It appeared so miraculous to me, and I wondered why I was not given the same beams of energetic power. He apparently came into this life with a different frequency of light, while I had my own, and did not have that same kind of energy. I was told that each of us bring in our own energy source to do the work that we have contracted with our guides to complete before incarnating into the Earth plane. My energy was on a lower frequency, so I could do the meditative work that I do. A feeling of calmness came over me and I immediately fell back to sleep.

The next morning I told Bert about what I had seen. A strange grin came over his face as he listened intently. It was as if on some level he knew, for when we first met, he told me that he was different, and now I was beginning to understand what that meant.

Earlier that day when I was observing the Crystal beings renewing their energy and I was told not to use their revitalizing machine, this helped me to have a better understanding that while we are all equal in the eyes of God, we also have different talents and energy requirements that suit our life purpose. I realized it was important not to judge ourselves or others, but to accept the beloved beings that we are, our own talents, strengths and power, and our own soul being. I was grateful for this lesson and to be able to move forward in my own power. In a flash I realized I was still on the Blue Crystal Planet and resting in one of their homes.

I felt the rush of energy as the gentle, pink feminine being sat down beside me focusing on my force field and asked me if I had rested enough. I replied that I had because the increase in light and strength was immediate, and I thanked her for her gift. She asked me if I wanted to visit yet another city and I enthusiastically agreed. Even though I had just experienced one of their timeless days, I felt refreshed as if I had received a night's rest.

CHAPTER TEN

A Visit to the Crystal City
and Reconnection with an Old Friend

"As I settled into an area of lovely, crystal formations and observed its inhabitants,
I experienced an awareness that the beings there, were so full of an overwhelming
comprehension of God, that it permeated my being profoundly with a
truly magical and marvelous consciousness."

I seemed, once more, to be soaring up, up, up, and going to another area of the Blue Crystal Planet. I had no idea where I wanted to go next. Darius showed me a holographic map of their planet which included its relationship to the entire universe. The map was complete in detail, and it was easy to follow, for the lights of each city blazed the way, and the one that I seemed to be heading toward emitted an exceptionally dazzling light. Although the Blue Crystal Planet was constantly illuminated, I still perceived a sense of darkness, and my guides automatically reflected the way for me, for which I was grateful.

Next, I sort of zoomed to a targeted city or gathering place on the grid. The colors jumped out as fuchsia hues and light pinks. My guide informed me as we slowly descended, "This is a gathering place where one comes to regenerate the Love of All There Is and is not only embraced by the Light, but also by a glorious awareness of Divine Love. It is highly refined and love of this frequency has not yet been expressed on the Earth plane. One would think that the greatest love was when humans find their soul mate, but this love far exceeds that. No one present on this planet is left without this awareness, and all are cared for unconditionally and equally. Once you feel this love, you can go to the various levels and feel higher frequencies and receive even more of a refinement of Divine energy. There are many levels of development among the beings in this city similar to others you have visited. These beings work on extending their ability to emanate and direct this intense frequency.

As I settled into an area of lovely crystal formations and observed its inhabitants, I experienced an awareness that the beings there were so full of an overwhelming comprehension of God, that it permeated my being profoundly with a truly magical and marvelous consciousness. They emitted an astonishing color and light that illuminated everything one hundred fold. They each reflected so much more of the crystal light than in the other areas I had visited. This fluid energy filled everything around them, and I could see a group transmitting opalescent rays in radiant streams to our planet. It was somewhat similar to the feeling I enjoyed on Earth when surrounded by the beautiful landscape or ocean scape and I experienced the love and peace that nature poured forth. This is why so many humans want to escape to the ocean, mountains, lakes, or woods because we feel this universal love and renewal.

Again, it is most challenging to convey this feeling or to communicate how they can manipulate their love energy to reach our planet, but they told me that the more humans open their hearts, the more it will be received. On the Blue Crystal Planet, no one needed to feel lonely. If we taught this awareness to all Earth beings, there would not be so much suffering or loneliness. There would not be suicide or killings or wars, for we would be so saturated with this love that we would only want to bask in it forever, and to reach out to others and share it with them. They told me I was accepted and loved by everyone on their planet and then some, out in the universe! It was a stunning revelation. They told me that they would infuse some of this love light frequency in me to take back to Earth. Then, I could share it with others and be able to infuse and assist them in integrating it into their physical bodies, minds, and souls. How wonderful was that?

This city just glowed and radiated out into the universe, and I could see its many rays and patterns oscillating and vacillating between the Earth and the Blue Crystal Planet. I was told that it was God's intention from the beginning to radiate this love to each soul on Earth and for mankind to receive it fully. Then the negative energies and forces interrupted the Divine Plan, and man put up barriers that somewhat limited their receptivity.

I wanted to see more about how this unique city was constructed. It was not like others in which crystal formations overlapped each other, but more spread out like a million lights with no end in sight.

A tall, feminine being approached me and asked if I would like to go into another vicinity of activity in this same city. I agreed, and this beautiful, radiating being allowed me to float in unified love until I reached another area, and, as usual, it was not divided into rooms, and I could immediately observe that it was some kind of chamber where they procured crystals. These were utilized in their love transmission work. This area was more defined in substance and she showed me the wonderful pink crystals of many facets and brilliance that they worked with. We, here on Earth, have to labor in the mines or with the rock formations to dig out, chisel and polish the surfaces of a crystal, which takes a lot of time and talent. There, it was in another form and they worked somewhat with their hands to acquire them, but the crystals were not structured like ours. They were like a group of feathers that spanned out into huge forms and felt ever so soft and light, yet they did seem to have some substance.

My guide then used her feather-like fan and sort of gripped the refined, pink crystal substance and somehow, using her mind, changed the atoms and manipulated them to create an object. She was creating a magnificent crystal for me! It was not like the ones we have, but of higher light frequency and form. I tried to grasp it, but it just gently floated into my ethereal hand. She was having a good time with me, because with her mind she changed the form easily right before my eyes. First, it was large and like a crystal rock, but lightweight. Then, she formed a crystal ball and told me to picture the crystal ball I had been given by Lee Johnson, who was my good friend on Earth before she passed into the heavenly realms several years ago. The being wanted me to take the image of her crystal ball back and superimpose it over the one from Lee. The being said she would teach me how to use it as a guide or readout instrument. She implied that there was much validity to reading crystal balls and I had a lot to learn.

Somehow, she had created a type of holograph of the Earth, and she said that I could use it for the good of all mankind. She also said that I could reach those loved ones that have crossed over, and then messages would be imprinted into my brain to share with others. She said that my friend Lee had been waiting for me to get this information so I would be able to use the crystal ball she had given me to see her and to communicate with her. My guide encouraged me, saying that this would make it easier for me to see, hear, and sense with my Earthly senses. I was grateful for this information and I honored these beings for what they did, and certainly, I looked forward to closer communication with my dear friend Lee.

My guide continued, "The gems, crystals, vibrant rocks, stones and other Earth elements contain certain spiritual vibrations that we transmit to the Earth which is why your people are beginning to become interested in them. When humans desire to choose a crystal for themselves, they need only to hold it in their hands and touch the chakras in their body to feel if it is the right one for them. They will know immediately which ones they need in their possession. The crystals not only contain information, but also healing and comfort, which is why ladies want to wear them on their physical bodies. Humans need to know that the vibrational forces are at work for them and will continue to teach about conscious awareness using Earth elements such as these."

I learned much more about the lives of these magnificent Blue Crystal beings, and I experienced a great longing to remain there forever, however, I felt the now familiar reminder of my guide that it was time to return to Earth. So, holding the vision of a crystal ball in my mind as I was directed to do, I allowed myself to return to my physical body and my consciousness to take in my surroundings. I felt refreshed and invigorated, and I looked forward to my day with Bert.

After a delightful outing with Bert that evening, I thought about my dear soul sister, Lee Johnson, who was mentioned to me during my earlier visit to the Blue Crystal Planet. Before she passed, she stated that she would try to contact me through her crystal ball that she gifted me. However, I had not had it out for quite some time. I asked myself if it were still possible for her to contact me in that way, as well as through this laptop computer that I was using at the present. I decided to try. There was an immediate, urgent response.

The words flowed rapidly and with ease. "Oh, Ethel, I have waited so long to hear from you. Sometimes I come to you in your dream state or sleep state. There is no time here, so it's hard for me to know how long we have been separated. Occasionally, I look in on you as I do my darling girls and Joel, my son.

"You cannot imagine how magnificent it is to be on what you call the other side. All souls here go to their designated areas or what they call their cosmic home. We are given a review of our life on Earth when we cross over and are oriented to our true selves and light bodies. We still have a connection to our conscious mind and can tune into what our thoughts and lives were when we experienced the planet Earth. There is so much out here, so vast and limitless.

"We first learned about our many past lives and accomplishments while on Earth. There were many, many journeys and challenges that we undertook. I do not have to undergo Earth life anymore, thank goodness. It is a difficult task, and we have to almost sacrifice ourselves to come down to this level of existence. We have so many choices to make along with our heavenly guides and angels. You would not believe the many billions of universes there are and the many life forms and energy forms and just plain unbelievable light!

"When I finally died, my soul just soared into the heavenly realms, and I saw the many angels that came with me. They were first around my bed. I am sure you remember me telling you about them. As I left my physical body, I felt an ecstasy and a love embracing me like I had never had on the Earth. I saw brilliant landscapes, flowers, and gardens that far surpassed those on Earth. Everything here is so full of life that each soul pulsates with love and light, and the colors are so vibrant that they would blind the naked eye.

"All my relatives and friends that had passed before me appeared, and we didn't need to say any words or ask questions. Communication came on a telepathic wave, and my mind was so clear, that I felt like all the heavens opened up to me.

"So much of the work on Earth that we did together was but a glimpse of what lies ahead for you. Tell your family, friends and all mankind that they do not have to fear death, for it is a marvelous adventure and so liberating to be free, free at last. Where I am now encompasses many levels, and we just use our mind to think what we desire or where we want to go, and manifestation is instantaneous. My former husband, Buck, did appear to me after I became better oriented. None of our wrongs or errors that we had on the Earth plane mattered. It was as if we first met and were so in love. This love continues, but in a more spiritual way.

"There is so much to tell you, but I have to reserve my electromagnetic energy so we are somewhat limited in our connection. Part of our work here is to bring the Earth back into alignment with the advancement of the rest of our solar system and into positive light waves. We also are involved in exploring space and other planets. Our guides encourage us to expand slowly as we traverse the numerous places so we will not be overwhelmed. Each of us has our guardian angels, guides and teachers sometimes one on one, and other times in groups. It took me a while to be able to transport my light body. I was flipping all over the place and everyone was laughing, but in a kind, understanding way.

"Tell my children that I am in the most glorious state and that I do check in on them. Share these words of comfort and tell them I send my love and much healing.

"Ethel, spend more time with me for we have great work to do again, together, only this time it is you on Earth and me on what you call the other side. I will try to explain more to you as we continue this journey. My best to your children and to Bert. By the way, my spirit name is Ohria and I have seen your magnificent guide, Anastasia. She is so gracious and such a kind being."

In a second she left, and I found myself back at my desk. That day I spent time with the crystal ball Lee had given me and as I had been instructed, superimposed over it the image of the ball from the pink being. Powerful light and energy emerged as I spiritually linked the two together. I looked forward to Lee's assistance, and that night I resumed contact with her.

She immediately responded as I typed.

"I am so happy and ecstatic that we are finally connected and communicating. I've been waiting for this for a long time in your timeframe. We have so much to accomplish together working from both sides of the veil. The beings who work with us are beginning to have more trust in the work that we are going to be doing together, and will give us more and more of what you may call sensitive information. They are starting to share their feelings, emotions and names with us and this will become more of a bonding process. They, too, feel the need for oneness with their planetary sisters and brothers.

"It is of paramount importance that you recognize the power of crystal gazing, which is more scientific than most people perceive. It is much like intuiting a microchip that is used in your computers and other electronic devices. I will not take time now to go into scientific principles here, but it is important for you to appreciate its powers. In time, you will be able to understand more of how images and symbols are transferred to your senses. As you know, it is a holographic universe and you will be working mostly with the fourth- and fifth-dimensions, Of course, the levels within each dimension are consistent with what you would call the square powers multiplied a million times. It is a simple, yet complex concept. Once you actually practice the crystal technique and become familiar with its powers, it will be easier to receive the necessary information that I want to share with you.

Crystals and crystal balls are extremely powerful, and when implemented in a positive manner they can bring up a wealth of pictures, symbols and information, unlike your modern technology. They require careful and precise care and maintenance, which I will now explain.

"First, clean your crystal with soap and water or vinegar, no chemicals, for that will distort the reflection and images that come through. Then you must ask for protection and guidance always, for there are entities out here that can intrude. Next, you must get permission for your guides and mine to work together for the connection. We still have many guides and teachers here as you do in your world. Then, in a calm manner ask that you and I enter into the crystal chambers on the Blue Crystal Planet. The Crystal Ball is a minute replica of how crystals operate.

"Now, when you align the grids between dimensions correctly, and you employ your cosmic or intuitive mind, you can transfer thoughts and objects into your consciousness through the crystal reflection as a result of its many complete prisms or facets. The facets of the crystal ball are considered 'complete' in that they appear as one smooth surface. This configuration emanates a higher energy level than a faceted crystal with points, and this allows people to more easily open the third eye and crown chakra to receive information. It reflects back the entire planetary system and infinite knowledge by connecting with the planetary grids.

"You can actually visit the planets in the solar system in this manner. If you focus on a certain name or person that lived on Earth and is now on the other side, they will reflect themselves to you in their entirety. You will see their greater selves as they truly are, and recognize them by their Earthly form, or they may have changed into their heavenly body. Information will be available through the apex of each complete facet simultaneously from the past, present, and future, which is why people who employ crystal balls are called fortune tellers because they receive information about the future.

"It is necessary to still and center your mind, body, and soul into one track and intend that your DNA encompass the light waves that can bring about form. At first, you will see hazy lines and then, when you refocus with your intuitive mind you will bring the lines together as to present the picture more clearly. I will focus from my side and modify the many dials I use to tune my light body form into a clearer human or physical vehicle, so you can recognize me as you did when I was on the Earth.

"However, I can also present my body as you knew it in an Egyptian past life when we were together working in the Temple of Healing using many alternative methods. At that time, the Earth inhabitants used crystal power in many ways and were able to heal their bodies, souls and the planet as well. In the future, I will relate more detailed information about this experience, so you can recapture and reawaken in your memory codes that took place many eons ago. Incidentally, these recollections are beginning to return now to many Earth humans who have reconnected to that era and sacred way. It will be positive information for you to use.

"We were also together in Atlantis where crystals were highly effective in providing energy and healing for that culture. However, you will remember that crystal power did become misused at the end of that cycle and ultimately resulted in their downfall. This continent is now being discovered under your oceans and in time, more of these truths will emerge.

"This information is so valuable and necessary, for we do not want to see the same mistakes repeated by the current Earth inhabitants, or they will destroy their planet and will have to regress and start at a lower place of evolution. Currently, the misuse of nuclear power needs to be eliminated, and if not, this too could cause much destruction. You have come too far for that to happen, which is why there are so many ambassadors on the other side willing to take on this task. I happen to be one of them, for I studied metaphysics for a long period on the Earth plane, which better enables me to converse with you.

"In addition, I also requested to be one of the White Brotherhood ambassadors for your planet. It will be necessary for me to transport myself to other dimensions and planets as well to receive more training to qualify for this arduous task. However, I made a commitment while in the physical to come back not in another physical body, but to use my light body and work through the many grids to do this work.

"You see, you and I knew that there would be much to accomplish from the Other Side to help the Earth align with the new paradigm, and it was true then, and now, even much more. However, what you call effort and hard work is made easy and effortless for us here. We do not have the physical to deal with, only our light wave energy forms that we can always regenerate or re-energize in a simple manner. We interact with the energies in a much different way, and this process is not easily explainable. Because we are not in a time element, our endeavors are quickly effective and powerful, with immediate results.

"Your part will be to cooperate and be available to bring this about, as you are doing right at this moment in the middle of your night. We are honored that you would do this even in your tired, physical state. We can regenerate you and help you with any medical problems, so you can maintain this type of energy so needed for us to continue the work.

Know that I work along with my guides, teachers, healers and angels as we align you with yours for practical interpretation of issues, so they can be understood and applied on Earth. We do have our limits; however, when either of our energies subside then we reconnect at another moment.

"I heard you talk to Kathleen on the phone this evening and intercepted on your behalf to assist this poor soul who was asking for guidance. This is the nature of the support that you will be affording others in their need or crisis. You will be implementing your intuitive powers, which allows us to connect and support you with the other side."

CHAPTER ELEVEN

More on Birth and Death on the Earth

"The inhabitants of our two planets not only intermingle freely with each other, but, also extend out to numerous solar and star systems."

I spent the next several days practicing my connection with Lee through my crystal ball. She projected a lively presence, and as I was counseling my clients she provided current information that was accurate and pertinent to their needs. When it was appropriate, she added comments related to the nature of life after the physical body was discarded. People were quite curious, yet fearful, and hungry for more understanding and questioned the mechanics of the process. Some wondered about returning to the Earth for more learning or reincarnation. Others wanted to continue a loving contact with their friends who had passed over, or at least be reassured that they were happy and moving on.

At the same time, my guides kept urging me to complete this crucially important book, and so I returned to my computer with renewed vigor. Several unfamiliar ethereal beings appeared, along with Darius, resplendent with glowing energy, and he introduced me to one of them as Argone. Argone informed me that he wanted to speak on the life and birth processes of Earth. Darius said this was obviously quite timely and purposeful, as it was consistent with the current subject that seemed to be coming up for a lot of people.

Argone vibrated like the Blue Crystal beings and was related to them, but he came from another culture on a planet named Aranius, which was in existence far longer than the Earth.

Darius explained, "Aranius is a sister planet to our planet and the Earth. These are extremely advanced, loving, heavenly beings that radiate much guidance, light, and love from the Celestial Sun as well as a direct connection to the Great Central Sun or God! The inhabitants of our two planets not only intermingle freely with each other, but also extend out to numerous solar and star systems. This is a difficult concept for you to understand in your terms, however, this is similar to your interaction between continents and, also, the oneness humans are striving to attain between their cultures on the Earth. Beings from both our planets are presently doing all they can to bring this about.

"Argon means 'Master of Creating or Creation.' He joins with us from time to time to plan a project that he and others from both planets decide together. In a similar respect, humans on the Earth get together with CEOs from other companies to work on projects that would improve the company or its employees to create innovative products or more prosperity and success."

I just listened in awe to the celestial concepts that most people on Earth never even think about. I observed the beings from Aranius. They glittered with yellow or golden tones, like the Asian peoples of our planet. Although light beings, I sensed that they could appear humanoid, if needed. Their golden hue blended well with the crystal beings and I noticed that when they infuse their colors together, they emit a strange but impressive blue and golden metallic sheen or radiance. When the two groups come together, there was such light and fragrance that I desired to absorb and bathe in this energy forever.

So it is with these various planets, their leaders, and their dynamic, extensive, advanced ideas as they fashion, design, and recreate. It is such a vast array of global planetary systems, solar galaxies, star constellations and so on—too complicated for me to understand at this time.

Argone, interrupting my thoughts, spoke, "Yes, we come to you on a light wave with a certain vibration and frequency. However, we know that your species communicates by way of name vibrations, so Darius gave you mine. Although I am androgynous, I have a more male substance or essence similar to your males. I also know that you communicate with Darius from the Third Galaxy. Darius is of a different dimensional level than us, but we do know of some of these beings for they work with the entire galactic system, and they do come to assist us or plan mutual projects as well from time to time. He is a master teacher in his own right. I am a master adviser on my planet, and we mainly deal with our environment and the Earth. However, I, too, can interact with other dimensions, and, now, I do have the arduous task of assisting mankind. I choose to do so, for they are especially dear to my heart.

"I wish to address the questions of Earth regarding birth and life on the other side or other realms beyond the Earthly third dimension that so many humans question. I do want to emphasize again that the birthing process for mankind is intentionally adapted to their species and environment. It is a difficult task to undertake for the soul Being that chooses to enter this plane from the other dimensions.

"Each entity must go through a type of orientation and course work so they will enter the dense habitat with a mission, theme, and purpose to complete for their soul development and growth. There are many reasons to incarnate and it may also simply involve the desire to experience the physical world and body as they perceive it. Also, there are many beings in the earth plane at this time who are reaching higher levels and come into the Earth to share the information with others. They have powers to heal in many modalities. Often they are simply helping the person to find within themselves ways to rebalance their energies. For humans are perfected beings in the sense that our souls are perfected and use the physical body vehicle to learn more and to explore and experience the earth. This includes exploring other dimensions and planets in the many billions of universes. When we say the soul is perfected we mean before it enters the Earth environment, because once it becomes an earth inhabitant, it then becomes mutated. That is, it becomes other than its perfected soul seed. It comes to experience this earthly realm, but believes that it can also perfect the Earth and become the fourth and fifth and sixth dimensional beings that it is or already was.

"So now, because the body vehicle is so dense and embedded in matter, the brain takes over to operate the body and its many functions, therefore, the physical brain limits the mind that is connected to the God Source and forgets where the soul came from and where it is going. This is often called the veil of forgetfulness. It is only when we begin to separate our brain and body from the higher self that it becomes aware of the cosmic mind and the greater 'I Am.' There are so many guides and advisers, counselors and teachers on the Other Side that assist in this process. Once the soul chooses to incarnate, he or she then decides with their guides which parents, energy spot or birth place to enter. Remember, there are also many negative energies to deal with on the Earth plane and there are mitigating circumstances that enter into the scheme of things that the soul has to deal with such as poverty, disease, drug addiction, bad relationships and more.

"Each entity is equipped with a code imprinted in their DNA that allows free will and they can make wrong decisions that are not in their contract as previously discussed and agreed upon by their master teachers and guides. However, they can call upon them at any given moment and help is on the way in the twinkling of an eye. In order to receive assistance, they must connect to their soul seed, or essence, or higher self in order to turn themselves around and return to their path. This is where other humans such as your doctors, therapists, counselors, friends and family can provide compassionate care.

"So, entities can get themselves into all kinds of trouble. There are those who stay the course, and their path, and have relatively easy lives to live while there are many that continue to struggle and fight for mere survival. This is an extremely difficult planet to live on in a physical or manifested form. It is also a high honor to come here and to do the things that one does. We look after our sisters and brothers of the planet much more than they can perceive. So, if they will open their minds and hearts to us, we can assist in ways that they will not be able to understand at this time. Know that there is help available at all times. Your Christ has not deceived or left them, and He works through many of his followers, masters, teachers, and counselors. The soul only needs to have the faith that things will work out in the Divine Plan.

"There needs to be a more global, unified vibration, for lack of better words, for assistance to the newborns when they enter your world. More outside workers, as well as family members, need to be available to surround these entities with love, light, and compassion through all their phases of life, growth and development. Then, there would not be feelings of loneliness, emptiness, or lack of love, and the necessary provisions for children would be present to nurture them not only physically, but also mentally and spiritually.

"Regarding the transition called death, there are many teachers, counselors, guides, and guardian angels to facilitate this process. Humans think that death is the end, but it is only the continuing of their God-given spirit. Once the soul leaves the body, it is released to the heavens, but it goes where the personality matrix believes it will go. For instance, if one believes that he will be joined with his Earthly loved ones, then these persons will be there. The Christ Light will be present, as well, to embrace one back home into loving arms, should the deceased personify Jesus or the Christ as the one meeting him. God is in many places and many beings, and has innumerable messengers and teachers along with the multitudinous angelic realms. Now, should one have a belief in His other messengers, like Mohammad and Buddha, he will be greeted by them. The personality matrix continues, for until you reach the ultimate truth, the individual soul is intact until it melds into the Oneness of His Being.

"Humans will begin to tie in the truths of all religions and the many cultures and diverse species on Earth as being in oneness. It is difficult to image this at this time, due to the negative forces in various parts of the Earth such as in Iraq, Iran, Turkey and other hot spots. However, when the United States realizes that it cannot impose its will on other countries and vice versa, then there can become a more meeting of the minds and it will be understood that each country has free will and can govern according to its own peoples.

"This is going to take a long time, for it will mean no more wars or conquering of territories. Mankind will realize that the land is for all people of all nations because God created the Earth to be owned by all in one accord and unison. We have to love and cherish all and be in unity for this to happen. This is the real teaching of the Christ, as well as other divine messengers who have been sent to the Earth. When we all can learn that we have differences and can respect these differences, then and only then, will humans see these desired changes. The Earth is going through a cleansing and purifying process at this time. There will be a lot more dramatic changes, but know that it is in the overall plan. Then, in these crisis situations, people will turn to a different way of believing.

"Entering the other realms after physical death may be perceived as a difficult concept, but humans need to remember that they are never left alone, and it is like walking from one room through the door into another room. For when the soul leaves the body, it is immediately greeted by light and love, and is reoriented to go to its destination. Even the most negative beings of Earth, such as those who harm others, are taken to a place of love and forgiveness. They do, however, have to pay the consequences of their behavior and learn not to repeat it, and they contract to come back to the Earth and continue to have the opportunities to learn their lessons.

"There is no physical Hell or damnation, for God is loving and merciful, as your Bible states. Souls are already saved, and you need only to become more in alignment, so you can become aware of who and what you really are. Salvation was meant for you to look within yourselves and your own universe to see the soul spark and to operate in the light. There is a place of redemption and purification where souls that have been truly disconnected from the source for eons of time, and had multiple opportunities to return to God, are taken to reorient themselves to return to the consciousness they had in the beginning of their soul journey. They are worked on by many guides, teachers, masters, and healers to bring them to an awareness of who they really are and their purpose in the universe. As with all souls, they review many of their past lives and wrong doings. Only in rare cases where the lesson is not learned must they spend time enduring repeatedly the consequences of their misdeeds. By this compassionate method, they learn how to develop a more sensitive conscience, and begin to recognize their oneness with their fellow mankind. They have time to meditate and contemplate their misdeeds, and must go through long periods of transgressions and forgiveness. Then, with growth, every soul is received back into the heavenly realms and is eventually redeemed by the creator as taught by the Master Christ.

"Also, keep in mind that God has numerous avatars such as the Buddha, Allah, and other master teachers on the Earth. Many paths and portals have been provided to receive divine knowledge, and it is critical to honor all religions. None have the ultimate truth, but humankind is not left without a variety of paths to reach enlightenment.

Some entities have a personality matrix with such a strong pull or attachment to the third dimension or Earth, that they have difficulty knowing that their physical body is no longer available, and that their soul essence has left it. That does bring on some confusion because in reality, they are in their ethereal bodies. They may perceive that they still have some unfinished business with family members or events on Earth, so they may hang around longer still attempting a physical expression.

If they have not developed spiritually during their life in a physical body they may cling to that reality, not understanding that other dimensions exist. However, their spiritual guides are always at their side urging them to go towards the light, but they may not acknowledge this for quite some time. They still have free will, and, so we have some Earth-bound souls wandering about, that are known as ghosts or apparitions."

I stopped Argon for a moment because I wanted to tell him about a recent experience I had that occurred at my daughter's house at 2:30 am.

"Argone, I had just gotten to sleep and I felt someone grab my right foot. At first, I thought I was dreaming, but then I woke up and someone still had hold of my foot. I kept trying to get it loose, but had difficulty. I did not see anyone. I just felt this large hand around my foot. I jerked and jerked until finally he let loose, and I even had a hard time kicking the cover off of me. I must say it gave me the creeps and frightened me so much that I went to my daughter's bedroom and woke her up. She, too, had experienced someone sitting on her bed that night. She even felt the imprint of the person on the bed. We now think it was the same man.

"We, then, went back to my room and sat on my bed and asked spirit who this person was and began sending him into the light with his angel guides. Suddenly, he communicated, giving me his name as Jeremiah and said that he was a slave.

"In my mind's eye, I saw a rather large, old, black man with sadly haunting eyes. He said he had been in darkness for a long time and when he saw my light, he came to me because he desperately wanted to leave. He realized that he was dead, but thought he was trapped. I told him not to be afraid, but to look into the heavenly Christ Light, and that his angel guides would take him to his heavenly home. I saw him leave and he looked back with a relieved expression and was blowing me kisses.

"He asked if there was anything he could do for me, and I quickly responded that I wanted to publish my book. He said he was with his Jesus and would ask Him to help me. He, then, began to name his family members as they came to greet him. He looked so happy and serene, and

I felt that I actually helped this person to cross over. He was so glad to go on to his heavenly home. He, in our time, had waited a long period and it was as if he was trapped here. This slave, Jeremiah, had lived a difficult life, and he was glad to be free."

Argon replied, "That was a clear case of someone who knew he was no longer in a physical body, and you did just the right thing to send him on to the light. However, it is a different phenomenon when loved ones peek in now and then to check on you or to give you messages or guidance. They realize who they are and where they are. They merely want to continue their path on the Other Side where they emanate positive energy, and offer guidance or send love and support to those completing their contracts on the Earth.

"When we see souls extend or disconnect from their dead bodies, they are carried upwards by their heavenly umbilical cord. This reaches to infinity similar to the physical umbilical cord, which is attached to one's mother at physical birth. This is cut for the purpose of allowing the infant to gain nourishment outside the womb. The being becomes an individual entity, and is dependent upon its mother and parents for physical, emotional and spiritual growth while in the Earth environment. Here, on the Other Side there is a vast web of cords likened to a spider web that is the soul attachment to the Godhead. Upon death, each individual soul has his own heavenly spiritual path and continues to travel along the web until his own light appears, and then follows it to his heavenly destination. This is a complex idea to explain, but in time more will be understood. In addition, these lines of energy or webs connect to the many planets, dimensions, and universes. It is true when the Christ said that, 'In my house are many mansions.' This is a simpler way to explain it.

"After leaving the physical body, the soul joins family and friends on the other side for a while, then moves on to experience his heavenly spiritual growth. You can picture this web, or matrix of webs as the silver cord that your Christ spoke about. This has millions of lights like a

Christmas string of lights all attached and held together. A safety net, so to speak, is provided so the soul never has to fear being alone, for it is always connected and surrounded by light and love with many guides and teachers along the way.

"When humans experience an out-of-body or near-death experience and see themselves going through a tunnel with a bright light at the end, they are actually traveling through their thread or cord. They cannot perceive the brightness around it, for it would be consuming, so it appears as though they are traveling through a dark tunnel. It is the outer limits or space that is dark, and the light is waiting at the end. However, during such an experience they are sometimes given the message to come back, and that it is not time to leave the Earth. This is the soul asking them to re-enter the physical body to complete the contract they have agreed upon. Then, they re-enter their body and have been given a glimpse of what it is like when they release their soul at a later time. This is truly a remarkable gift.

"Then, there are humans who release their physical body early in life because they have gone as far as they want to with their current Earth lessons. The timing to do this is similar to a person who attends college and enrolls in a four-year course and decides that is enough education, so he stops there. There are others who feel that they must get a master's or a doctor's degree or even more, so they stay and acquire more knowledge. Because souls have free will, they have the authority to make such decisions.

"I do want to mention that some souls after death choose to remain close to the Earth for a duration of time and act as spirit guides or teachers to humans that they love, or are even assigned to assist."

I knew just what Argon was talking about because Bert and I had long ago had a most spiritually expanding, initial encounter with our spirit guides. We were spending our anniversary celebration at Blackwater Falls, West Virginia.

It was a cold, winter day when we decided to take a walk in the forest near the inn where we stayed. We were immediately surrounded by a herd of gracefully, grazing deer, and we watched them quietly as we sat on a snowy bench. All of a sudden, we felt ourselves bathed in breathtaking, golden light. We easily drifted into a meditative state, and were given information about our Earthly spiritual guides. I sensed that my guide, Anastasia, had always been with me, but I was given her name for the first time. Bert knew that he, too, had always been guided and that things always came easy for him. However, he did not know who his guide was and the name that came to him was "Timothy." The vibration felt so right for him, and, immediately, he began to receive messages for both of us.

We were told that we had a higher calling, and that we would be working together spiritually to help others to connect to their higher selves and to their inner soul being. Since we were soulmates, we had been together before in many lifetimes, and it was essential in this life that we serve others and help them know their true selves through the many lessons placed before them. We were given information on topics for workshops that we would conduct in the years that followed, which included knowledge about the planets and star systems. There was even a reference made to the book I would publish about the Blue Crystal Planet. We truly had an enlightening, magical encounter, and the very positive contact with our guides continues to evolve.

Argon nodded in approval of my explanation, and remarked, "Human-kind, who are not yet fully aware of where their guidance comes from, will be amazed at the numerous, unseen spirit beings who humbly and lovingly serve them, and usually are never identified, nor receive credit for their assistance. When they realize that stepping out of the physical body is just like walking through an open doorway into another room, the veil between dimensions will gradually thin, and as their frequency rises, the veil would completely disappear, and they will see their guides! This will happen as mankind progresses."

I listened to him and was curious, and interjected, "But Argone, tell me why we so fear death and why we cannot be comfortable with the process of integrating into the higher dimensions?"

"Earthlings fear death because they are only familiar with their current, present conscious level. When they become aware of other realities and decrease the patterns of constant distraction and mind chatter, they will know more clearly who, why, and what they are. Humankind usually only experience the physical level, and their five senses because they are focused on the solidity of things or conscious moment which is the illusion of the third-dimension. They are much more than they deem themselves to be. It's as if they are painting on a canvass and their focal point is primarily on what they are painting. This is why psychics are called intuitive, due to their ability and lack of fear which permits them to focus simultaneously on the past, present, future, as well as other dimensions at the same time. But remember, there is no time or space on the other side, and these concepts are only the constraints of mental conditioning and Earth consciousness. Psychics are gifted to move past this barrier and receive information in a timelessness arena, our universe.

"If humankind will allow their consciousness to expand, they will experience many realities, and there are some who allow themselves to disregard Earth illusions and remember past abilities or tap into other realms for inspiration. These are considered protégées, such as Mozart and Beethoven who created symphonies at a young age. This, again, is difficult to explain, so we use the tools of communicating that we have at the present moment.

"The dimensions on the other side are so glorious that humankind might think them unbelievable! If you imagine the most beautiful painting you have ever seen and then magnify it a thousand times, then you might be close to the beauty and composition. The colors are indescribable, for you do not have these colors on the Earth plane. They are much brighter, have more hue, more richness, more depth than any you have ever seen in any picture, flower, or cloth. The greens are intense green-

green; reds are red-red and so on. It is almost impossible to describe them, unless you have experienced being in the higher dimensions. Of course, because you visited the Blue Crystal Planet, you know what I am talking about.

"Structures in form are also splendid in the higher dimensions and mimic the architecture of humankind. We have structures of every type, including classical Greek, or Roman-period buildings. There are huge forums in which to listen to lectures and view the arts, and tremendous libraries and research centers to gather and expand knowledge. In addition, there are individual homes and smaller buildings for general use and beautiful fountains, plazas, courtyards, and parks, as well as gardens and meditation areas, are abundant.

"All the descriptions of a utopia world would not be enough to describe the beauteous realms of the Other Side. When in the eternal heavens, one never can run out of topics or things to learn or discuss, for there is an infinite cosmos out there, full of millions of stars, planets, and galaxies, and it is impossible to know it all, as more is constantly being created. It is, indeed, a paradise!

"Of course, there are numerous souls that cannot wait to come home to this heavenly realm, and to the arms of their Heavenly Father. People are constantly bathed in love, and light, and feel so free. There are no strangers, and individuals are not only with their Earthly family and friends, but the heavenly hosts of angels are always at your side."

Argon was complete in his discourse and, with a loving farewell, vanished before my eyes. I reflected on the amazing joy and beautiful experiences that awaited humans on the other side, and had much gratitude for my experiences, as a clairvoyant which allowed me to catch a glimpse of this reality.

There have been many accounts of near-death experiences where people have returned to their bodies and related what it was like on the other side. In addition, many of our dreams, or even daydreams, are visits to other dimensions.

Such was the time I had in an encounter with my older sister, Betty Gall, who, at the time, was living in her human body in Ohio. I was awakened by her presence one night, and urged to go to my computer. She seemed to be above me, and said, "Hi, this is your sister. You should see where I am. I'm in such a beautiful place in the heavens. I am looking down and can see you. Junior, (another name for Bert) is here, giving me a tour like he always did in D.C. I see Mom and Dad and remember them as if I were a child. They look so young and bright in their new bodies.

"Gosh, you guys on Earth look funny! You look like you are wrapped in bubbles of blob and move so slowly. The heavenly beings showed me how I look on Earth on a type of screen, like a holographic picture. I am a large blob who can hardly move my bubble of blob. I hate how I look and feel, and it is so great to be out of that type of body here. I didn't realize how miserable I felt on Earth until now. Here, I am light and quite beautiful. I see Grandma, Grandpa, Batua and Nenya, too. Also, the boys and Irene are around. They had a huge party celebration with magnificent, angelic beings, and sang for me with music like I have never heard.

"Your music sounds out of tune and discordant. You guys better practice more to get harmonized with the rest of us here. We move around fast because we sort of think different than you in this bright light. We merely think wherever we want to be, and are instantly there. It is so much fun to explore the worlds. We don't have to talk, we just put it out, and others can do a read-out. I am just learning so much about where I am. It's incredible!

"When I look in on you and see you walking and talking, it looks weird to me. You guys have to work so hard. It looks like slow, slow motion from my vantage point, as if it takes forever to just exist on planet Earth. Don't take me wrong, because you do think that is the way it is, and your Earth is beautiful, but compared to where I am, it is quite different.

"I can make music with my piano here—unbelievable to you, for I just pull my vibrations together, and there it is. It's absolutely harmonious, and blends with these beautiful beings. Each of us look the same, sort of, but with our personal frequencies we look different to each other. No one judges how we do things, or look, or the way we choose to continue to learn about the many planets and universes. To you, these look solid, but here they are made of a soluble material, and you can see and move through them exceedingly easily. It is hard to explain, but when you sleep or go into a high frequency, you can catch visions and hear with your light body what I am trying to describe.

"Boy, I don't miss the conflicts and discord with my Earthly family and others in your world. It seems so strange to hear people always talking, talking, talking about bad things. Here it is so positive, and the light and love by all beings is something I have never experienced before. They did show me times I had been on Earth, but call them previous lives. Actually it is like a play or just scenes from one to the other, or chapters in a book.

"By the way, Ethel, you need to complete your book to share it with as many people as you can, so they can learn or remember what and who they were, and about other beings and planets.

"It looks funny when you step out of your blobby bodies, for in this place we look crystalline and pure, but not yet complete, as we really are. There is a lot I have to share with you, but I can feel your vibration slowing down and you need to rest yourself. We will talk more later in your time. Tell Lilly and the family I am unbelievably fine. Ken will join me in a while. I am so glad that you do not shut yourself down like many others on Earth, and I can communicate with your bright light, and that you are so open to me, and so forgiving, and know that we are now soul-sisters. I love you with all my heart and being. Take good care of yourself and hear me often. You have much to teach others as they also teach you, and we give you the knowing of all that is.

"By the way, they call us heavenly sisters and brothers. We are androg-ynous and sort of blend into each other. Tell Cherrie she is doing the right thing, and it will bring much happiness to her. She is right. It takes a lot of faith to bring blessings into your lives. Bye for now. Love you!"

Even though my sister was still in an Earthly body, she was obvi-ously having experiences preparing her for her time to leave. It is most comforting to know she is already beginning to adjust well to her new dimensional environment. And so it is with all Earth beings demonstrat-ing that much joy and freedom awaits us.

CHAPTER TWELVE

*Divine Blueprints of the Blue Crystal Beings
and the Earthlings' Cosmic Identity*

*"Darius explains the divine blueprints of the Blue Crystal beings
and how they differ from Earth beings."*

Tonight was Friday. Bert was sound asleep, and there was so much information floating in my mind, that I felt guided to go to my computer and really didn't know where to begin.

Darius, in a bright, golden flourish, tuned into my receptivity, wanting to give me more information. He reminded me that their planet was just recently discovered in our galaxy by our scientists. It has always been there, of course, but we, on this planet, are slow to rediscover.

Darius enthusiastically continued as I listened and typed, "The Blue Crystal Planet appears not to hold any third dimensional life forms. However, there are masses of bodies of water and land, but in a higher dimension and structure. Our beings do not need water to sustain themselves, because they get their sustenance from the atmosphere and environment that is conducive to their existence. They have a different molecular structure, and are composed of an activated DNA helix that is twelve-pronged. Although they are light, almost transparent beings, they have the power to manifest as bodies similar to the physical state, and when they choose, as mentioned previously, can change in a twinkling of an eye, and seem to disappear when you see them with the naked eye, usually in your peripheral vision. We think the blue print of what we desire to manifest, and, then, it just forms and manifests. If there are discrepancies, we merely alter or modify, using our cosmic mind powers, and readjust, and it's done."

I interrupted, "Darius, please stop for a moment, as what you are saying reminds me of an experience I had in 1977 and I want to tell you about it."

He nodded, and motioned for me to continue.

"It was after I completed my Master's Degree at UNCC and I accepted a position as Director of Kindercare. One day, a lady came in to register her child for daycare. She was quite tall, with dark hair, and a metallic type of voice almost like a recording within her physical body. I was told by my guides not to look directly in her eyes. I could tell by my peripheral vision that she had red pupils. He son was also large and tall for his age of five years.

"During the course of the day, there was much confusion and havoc with her son, whose name I do not recall. He seemed to not have any social skills, and was pushing the other children around to the point that they were fearful of him. We then had to put him in a small room by himself with a staff worker looking after him. She gave him some toys and books to play with, although he did not know quite what to do with them. It was, indeed, a long day.

"When his mother came to pick him up, we told her that it will take some time for him to adjust. She paid me cash for the day and said they would be back. I got the feeling that there were not of this world, and that they were here to experience and observe.

"The staff workers came out with her son, and we all watched as they went out the front door, across the yard and towards the apartments where she said they lived. All of a sudden like a flash of light, they disappeared into thin air. The workers were amazed at what they saw, as was I, for we had never seen anything like it before.

"Then, I went back to my office to look up the address on her registration form. I decided to call the manager of those apartments, and they looked in their records, and did not have anyone listed by that name, or any description of this tall lady and her son. We all decided that they were not of this Earth and were quite amazed. The staff also noticed that the son's voice was clearly metallic, as well. It was a true and unforgettable experience for us all."

Darius hesitated for a moment and then said, "Yes, obviously that was a being from another dimension wishing to experience some time on Earth; however, I do not think she was from the Blue Crystal Planet."

"Nevertheless, this brings me to another point. The more advanced souls of the Earth often transfer in their sleep state to the Blue Crystal Planet to receive information which they bring back to their waking, conscious state. That way, they can learn to align in their light bodies, or on a higher frequency, which develops the ability to think and function in the light. As the inactive DNA structure awakens in humans, the ability to release out of third dimension is heightened. Your scientists are beginning to realize there is much more to the helices of the DNA molecule than previously understood, and eventually they will be able to go further with this discovery.

"Remember, your Christ said, 'All things are possible, and what I do, you can do also.' As an advanced soul, He learned about living in the light well before He incarnated, and brought His experiences and knowledge in when He embodied. He was able to contemplate for forty days and nights to bring this light more fully into the world. Christ was clairvoyant, and performed numerous miracles. These gifts are available to all who choose to use them, and are not evil or dark, as some religious leaders teach, but a positive attribute of your total being. If all would meditate and contemplate as He did, there would not be the dark forces present on the Earth because humans would be operating only in the light, and would transmute all negative energies.

"So, just start with meditation and be open. Don't fear, for your angel guides are always with you to protect you and to allow you to go as high as you wish. It is in this light wave phase that you can heal yourselves, receive higher information, write, paint, and have musical abilities that you did not think you ever possessed. However, some of these abilities were partially developed in other incarnations and you bring them to the present to advance even further.

"The Blue Crystal Planet beings are given the task of helping each other evolve, as well as assist your species. They live in a parallel dimension to your planet, so they can infuse their light, knowledge, wisdom, and healing to you. That is why some of you might ask how it is that some Earth beings can be so insightful and intuitive. Sometimes it is a gift of awakening an ability from the Blue Crystal beings, since the individual has always, inherently, possessed this ability. The Blue Crystal beings connect with your ethereal selves, and then infuse stimulating information into your physical minds and brains. It is similar to filling up an empty vessel. They have the ability to transfer thoughts, because they already think in the light, so you can receive light waves that carry knowledge. This is similar to a microchip that carries stored information, music, or other communication.

"So, it is now time to wake up from your sleep and become aware of who you really are and your purpose in the Earth plane. You may have heard of the book, *The Ascension*, by Michael Carrroll. Take a good look at it, because it correlates with the Bible. As discussed in this book, there will be those humans who will be able to use their light bodies and transfer themselves to the higher realms. Then, there will be those who will still be encased in their physical bodies who will remain behind to have more opportunity to evolve.

"When Christ said, "I am the Light, He literally meant that He came as a messenger to save the world for without Light and the teachings of how to live on this planet, we would not exist as the human species, nor would the many creatures, trees, and the general environment. Unfortunately, much of His teachings were misinterpreted by the human race, and you do not have the correct awareness of His intent. The religions do have a kernel of truth, but there is no hell or damnation, but only light and stages of perfection in the afterlife beyond this Earth."

As Darius was speaking, my mind drifted to an experience I had with Bert where I had an exquisite and awakening encounter with the light, which changed me forever, and seemed to be in accord with what Darius was saying.

I interrupted him, as I just had to express the amazement I felt when I received this greater awareness of the high frequency of light, and tell him that I had an inkling of what he was talking about now. "Darius, please wait! I just must tell you about a time I experienced an intense interaction with the light that changed me forever."

Darius hesitated and waved me on to speak.

"Bert and I were skiing in the mountains of West Virginia and while walking in the snow in our ski gear, we were guided to go up a path to the top of Afton Mountain. As we neared the top, we sensed a heightened change in the energy emanating from the area and looking at each other in bewilderment; we continued on and discovered a palatial building that we did not know existed. A sign said, 'Swannanoa Institute.' There was no other car in the parking lot as we approached the porch of this mansion, and we could see a blazing fire in the fireplace, so we knocked on the door. A small waif of a girl with red hair answered and said that we could come in and tour the museum of Walter and Leo Russell. We had not heard of them before, but quickly viewed the many things collected in the museum.

"We found out that they had written many books such as, *The Man Who Tapped the Secrets of the Universe, Love and the Iliad*, and many others. They taught about ancient wisdom and how to live and think in light, and the information was fascinating to us. We saw other collections such as Mark Twain sculptures and also many documentaries and books authored by them.

"When we finished touring the museum, we were led to the great living room, and told to sit and warm ourselves by the fire. When we looked into the eyes of the tour guide, she looked like an old soul. She said she had lived there and worked for the Russells for many years. She explained that Walter Russell was twenty years older than his wife, Leo, and made his transition several years ago. Leo still lived in the upstairs of the palace and was continuing her writing. Then, looking up, we saw her coming down a massive staircase, and as she greeted us warmly, she took a seat next to us.

She exclaimed, 'You know, it was not by accident that you found the path to this sacred place. It is meant for those who seek the light. You will never be the same after this experience."

She, then, told us about her extraordinary husband and his many spiritual and creative gifts. He never graduated from college, but had received honorary degrees, and was invited to travel all over the world including visitations to the White House, and by other dignitaries in Europe.

"We were immersed in such tremendous and uplifting light from being in her presence and in the high frequency of the Institute. We gazed outside where there were remnants of beautiful gardens in the snow and huge, magnificent sculptures that overlooked the mountain made by both she and her husband. We noticed statues of the Christ Master and the Virgin Mary, among others. Leo paused, noticing our attention focused out the huge window. After a few minutes, she said that she and Walter traveled the world over to find this blessed, sacred place, and that many scientists, celebrities, dignitaries, clergy-men and other seekers visit from all over the planet.

"Leo hugged both of us before we left, and we felt so blessed and grateful that we had stumbled upon this heavenly place. Being there was a true awakening for us, and an unforgettable journey, and we were forever touched, and from then seemed to function in a higher frequency simply by being in the brilliance and warmth of the light of Swannannoa Institute."

Darius commented, "That is an amazing story, because although there are many sacred areas upon your Earth, many people miss them because they are not tuned into the frequency that will guide them there.

"The Crystal beings have the ability to remain tuned into the higher frequencies of light permanently, and that is why they are aligned with the Earth and are directing and teaching how to make the necessary changes for a 'Heaven on Earth.' That is why they do not have destruction and chaos on their planet as does the Earth. It is a slow process, because yours is a timed, linear dimension and theirs is not. They operate in the moment, and the now, and there is no time, for they have eternity and are aware of this."

"How, then, can we become more aware and learn to live in a higher frequency of light like your beings?" I queried.

He answered, "Well, first, humans must learn to slow down the static in their environment. This means learn to work with energies. Fortunately, many of your species are working with their frequencies and balancing the physical body and the Earth environment. This is challenging, for in one sense they must slow down and connect to their soul level, but at the same time, allow their molecular structure to speed up faster than the speed of light. When man is stilled, and not overcome with all the static and shock waves present in your culture on a continual basis, he becomes the true self that he is, and begins to remember where he came from and what his soul purpose is on Earth.

"Once this is accomplished, then, more work can be done with the changing of the molecule structure, such as bringing in or adding to their individual DNA. This is why your crime analyzers can identify a person with his DNA because each human comes into the third dimension with a specialized imprint. Each person is individualized because of his free will to make decisions on how to live in the Earth environment. The entire DNA is not yet activated, so, therefore, they are not as advanced as they could and will be. The cloning process will teach much about how humans are structured and how they can manipulate their actual being.

"Secondly, humans need to understand the power, methods, and positive use of directing energy. Beings on the Blue Crystal Planet have the capacity to devise and engineer their world by manipulating energies in order to get the desired results. Their environment consists of total light and color, and is effervescent. Their buildings and streets are made of varying light speeds so as to reflect the God Light. They can use thoughts in light waves to bring about their structures into a type of blueprint. They then, work together in teams on the same mind level to fill in the spaces similar to connecting lines. They construct effortlessly and do not require solid materials, for they have the ability to travel through these structures as they fine tune them. An analogy would be in order for humans to get inside their buildings, they have to have doorways in which to enter with their physical bodies. Cars require doors and space inside for humans to enter.

"The crystal beings only have to enter their structures with their energy embodiments or light bodies. When humans want to be at the beach, they can picture this in their mind, and they are there without the physical body and they call this a daydream. They cannot take their bodies there with thought, and they have to make a physical way to get there. Your species works with great difficulty to move around in their environment. The crystal beings have only to think in their light, change the molecular structure, and they are there. This is why humans would not be able to see them with their naked eyes. This is why they are called advanced beings, and they are already in heaven, or carry a part of heaven with them. This was intended for the Earth to have, when God created it, and, as well, heavens and billions of other planets, existences, and universes.

"These beings work in groups or on an individual basis. As they work and exert their energies on a light wave all in one accord, then they can hold the manifestation as long as they wish, or for infinity or eternally. They also have the power to cancel it or modify the manifestation, but it has to be decided upon by all that are involved in the project. They do not have conflicts for all decisions are made by the group with respect for each other's opinions and for the betterment of their well-being.

"In your world, decisions are made by a few in power and there is conflict and disagreement by the masses which puts the vibration in static form, and not in a harmonic blend. There is often the human error, and the imperfections of misplaced, misused energies working, which creates disharmony. Humankind call it the devil's influence, when it is really that they are working against their own spirit. When mankind focuses on a negative thought enough, it can manifest into what they call evil things or beings. In the future, you will be able to identify these thoughts that become things, and will learn to discern the negative thoughts and replace them with loving kindness and respect for all mankind and its creatures.

"This takes a more global view of your world, such as eventually allowing each nation to govern itself according to its own beliefs and cultural conditions. After this is accomplished, each nation will then have to take the responsibility of working and managing together its needs of caring for each other, including such issues as housing, clothing, health care, and employment, but it has to be for the betterment of the whole, and not for greed and selfish reasons. This will take a long time in Earth time constraints, but we and other beings on other planets and dimensions are willing to give humans the light waves of positive energy and the formulas for uplifting spirit and conscious levels in order to achieve this.

"We want to see our brothers and sisters become more lighted beings with the love, light, and power to enable themselves to live in harmony, peace, and love. Each one can teach others to love, but even more importantly, humans need to instill the ability to honor their own soul being, for that is what is considered to be the image of God, who is the creator of All That Is.

"Actually, each human comes into the Earth on a ray of energy and is coded with a type of frequency. So, when they desire to tune into the cosmic energy or the divine, they just tune into their own frequency and they will get the information they request, be it healing, education, inspiration, or desire for prosperity, happiness, and more, but they need to know how to tune into themselves. It would help to think of a note that you resonate with and sing it out with your voice and listen to it. Now, think it in your mind so you can hear it within your inner ear, so it connects with mind, body and soul. Then, listen and receive. This is what the Christ meant when he said, 'Be still, and listen, or know.'

"Each entity has been coded with this frequency which is similar to their DNA. There are also group codes. Sometimes humans read or sing together in unison in harmony. When this happens, they are tuning into the group code, so as to bring oneness or strength to each other. In doing this they must tune out the negative vibrations, and only enter in the positive, so to become pure as channels. When a human recognizes their own tone, they then can learn to tune into others. Ethel, you do this when you do readings. You align yourself with the other person's ray, or tone, and then receive information that is beneficial to that person.

"Humans can do this by listening or doing psychometrics. You have to dial in and keep turning the dials in your higher mind and then listen until it feels right or resonates with yours. When the human species can do this in a deliberate manner, they can conquer the obstacles that hinder their progress. When they can clear the static, they will not have to deal with unclear channels, and will better understand all mankind. This will enable them to begin to understand their thinking, feelings, their levels, their energies, what they can learn and understand. This is a far cry from trying to communicate in the way that mankind has been communicating for centuries. Other teachers have gone before you who have received similar teachings on the various rays. We can give you more information and methods to receive this information, including the meanings of the rays, their frequencies and colors, how to identify them, how they are coded, and how to use this knowledge in their every-day lives."

Darius slowed his pace of speaking and seemed to be concluding his teaching. He remained silent for a few minutes, and I sat contemplating his description of all the human race had yet to assimilate and accomplish. He then seemed to adjust his frequency, and I observed the radiant colors in his immense aura take on a much more golden hue.

Then he spoke, "Although what I have described seems mind boggling, allow me to take you for a brief glimpse of an even more amazing state of consciousness, one you have never experienced in your journeys to the Blue Crystal Planet up until now. You have, however, experienced this frequency between lifetimes and it can be accessed in your sleep state. This is a heightened aspect of our planet that I would like you to experience, so you will understand and recall in your conscious awake human state that even higher, mystical attainment is available."

I nodded in agreement and before I could think, Darius zoomed me up to a level of frequency I had never encountered before in past tours. I began to sense a euphoric, almost intoxicated sensation that was impossible to describe. He told me it was the seventh level, although I did not know what that meant. It was as close to utopia as one can imagine, and a display of the most delightful colors and fragrances was enveloping me. Amazingly, all my negative thoughts and feelings were erased and I embraced a sensation of being a clean, pure, translucent slate.

I seemed to be embracing a new experience, yet a part of me remembered that I had been there many times and it was as if I had finally reached home again. It was the sensation of a familiar, beautiful, haven, and I greeted it with immense joy. The beings there were like pure crystal, and although I saw colors, the primary energy seemed to be nothing but bright light, but not blinding light. It was as if my whole being was opened up, literally, and my mind expanded with the belief that I could write a hundred books or see a hundred movies at one time, or feel a thousand feelings simultaneously. It was an incredulous pleasure, and I could fathom the mysteries of the entire universe all at once, and have infinite knowledge. This was being as close to God, or our great creator, as I could be at that moment. I recognized how humans are neophytes and simply do not have this kind of understanding. I knew, then, what is meant like when we cross over or reach the Other Side in the heavenly realms.

The beings did not have to explain anything to me, for I understood them in their knowledge and wisdom, and felt like one of them for the first time, or like all of them at once. How incredible! They wanted me to experience this for myself, and to share this with many others. Here in this realm it is pure light, and a pure, yet, deeper love, not of oneself, but for the entire, universe, or even for what we would call all humankind. Here, they do not worry about structures, houses, books, libraries, or the way of transport, for here, one has all knowledge, infinite wisdom, and one's needs are entirely met. In other words, there is no need, but only being and oneness of eternal bliss. This is one of the highest levels there is and, yet, one may traverse the many universes to experience even more.

These beings seemed to all merge into one, and when I looked at them they were one group soul. As I observed further, it seemed as if there was an immense spread of light, or wings like angel wings, that fanned out as far as the eye could see. These were the angel wings that man has caught glimpses of from time to time. They could reach out into the universes and become a protective shield. The beings told me to call on them should we need protection or guidance, for this is their task. It looked like soft white feathers, but Darius told me is was actually softened light waves formed together as one. It was a magnificent sight to see, so full of glory and honor of the God source.

Darius explained that when these beings have completed a task as a group soul, they then returned to this dimension and began the process of separating out and again becoming more individualized. He said that together they do wondrous work, or what we would call miracles. They are the angels that save planes, cars, from what Earth people would call disasters. All we needed to do was to call on them. They will respond in a twinkling of an eye for they are the eyes of God. There was so much there for my brain to assimilate, but they told me they can help me grasp all of this. It was so much more colossal than I had ever imagined, and, yet, we can learn about this even before we cross over or leave our earthly bodies by meditation, and allowing ourselves to experience such phenomena.

With a gentle descent, I was reluctantly directed back to my office and the familiarity of my Earthly home. Darius guided me every step of the way, and now stood beside me as I harmonized my energy with my surroundings.

When I was somewhat acclimated, he spoke. "I sincerely wanted you to experience a taste of one of the most high heavenly realms," he quietly explained, "because it is important that you appreciate firsthand the energy that you are going to be writing and talking about to other humans. As the frequencies of the Earth continue to rise toward the higher dimensions, people are going to want to know firsthand what they are working towards, and how it feels to exist in these higher frequencies. Most importantly, they will want to meet someone who has consciously experienced it. There will be all sorts of questions, and you will be well equipped to answer them.

"It is highly important for humans to remember that each of them is a unique individual. Each comes into the Earth with his or her own exclusive vibration which is his cosmic identity, and it is his finger print, or DNA. Included with his personal ray are not only sounds but the many billions of color vibrations, most of which cannot be seen with the five senses. These rays of vibrations connect the human with their soul brothers and sisters, which is why they are drawn to those entities that they feel comfortable with. It also helps to direct them to the ones they need to work with, socialize, and, be in relationships with to complete their contract of experiences while incarnated on Earth.

"Humans are not always aware that there are moments and pauses in their embodiment and environment where all things are suspended, and they are truly in their actual light bodies. In truth, because God created humans in His own image which is multidimensional, the human physical form is only necessary when we use this vehicle to express God in the third dimension.

"In addition, humans and most beings beyond the third dimension are also multitudinous, meaning having innumerable, or limitless ways to express. This means humans can incarnate in physical bodies, as well as inhabit their heavenly homes. This is how they can meet with loved ones when they cross over, and yet, they can be operating in physical bodies on the Earth plane, as well as light bodies or points of light in other dimensions. Of course, the blue crystal beings have the ability to operate in your dimension as well as theirs. It's like being in two places at the same time. Remember, there is no time element on their planet so they operate simultaneously.

"These crystal beings are composed of the helix, and can function more rapidly than humans, for their molecular structure is of an unimaginable speed and is faster than the velocity of light. Their chemistry goes beyond your law of physics, and humans must be able to advance and evolve to understand this reality. Earth scientists are working on it as we speak. One day, you will look down on your human species, and will see light beings operating in a positive light and a highly advanced world. You must begin to visualize your world as unlimited and not restricted.

"There are many human species that are literally locked in their bodies, and can't seem to see the light, which is why it is so important for you to share these deeper truths and knowledge. There will be many parts of the world that are not ready to advance. You must work with the ones that are ready, and with the many masters that now circle your globe.

This is all for now, we will speak again soon."

With a gradually diminishing image, and a loving farewell wave, Darius began to fade into the distance through the wall of my office. No sooner had he disappeared, when the room became ablaze with the presence of Clarius, whom I had spoken to before. I acknowledged his presence and welcomed his bright, positive energy.

"Well, this is a surprise," I whispered.

Clarius spoke in an enthusiastic manner, "I have been listening to Darius speak to you, and have but a few short thoughts to add to the subject he was conversing about. I love to entertain new ideas or concepts for mankind, but keep in mind these concepts are not new at all but only a remembrance and re-connection to what you already know and what is coded in your soul seed. So, it's time, now, to nourish the soul, and allow it to blossom in accordance to the original blueprint that it had inherited eons ago from the God Source and that which was given or gifted to mankind.

"It is a beautiful gift to begin the journey of remembering who you really are, where you came from, and your mission and destination. After all, that is what mankind is continually searching for through its many religions, beliefs, scientific and philosophical ways.

"Each entity that is coming to Earth has its own cosmic blueprint or imprint. Each one comes on a specific soul frequency wave. The soul enters through biological birth, and chooses its own parents and environment in which to experience life in a solid or physical form.

"The Blue Crystal Planet has already evolved to higher dimensions, which allows the beings there to choose elevated experiences. We are in what you might call an enlightened or blissful state of being, which is why we are contacting and communicating with those who desire to receive us, and assist them in their reconnecting with their cosmic memory, or coded, seed soul. We are assisting numerous humans at this time, and all they have to do is ask, and we will be there to support and guide."

Clarius appeared to be complete in his speaking for the moment, and I needed to rest, so he bid me farewell and disappeared as rapidly as he had arrived. I had much to think about, and felt the urgency to communicate all this information as soon as possible to the people on the Earth.

CHAPTER THIRTEEN

Revelations of the Artistic Realms

"We are all instruments of God, and it is important how we use these instruments which should always be for the good of oneself and the highest good of all others."

It was Monday morning at 5:30 a.m. and I had a deep urge, almost a push, to come to my computer to write. It was October 22, 2007. It started when I heard in my mind that I must receive information about the inspirational music of the heavenly spheres. This energy seemed to be connected with our dear friend, Skip, who made his transition less than a week ago. Heidi, his wife, had an uplifting memorial service held at the First Presbyterian Church in Weaverville, NC. It was a marvelous event filled with music and celebration of his life.

Skip came into this world with his head and heart filled with music. He was an accomplished pianist, singer, director, and composer. He loved jazz and played for some of the great singers of his time such as Frank Sinatra, Mel Torme, and Ella Fitzgerald, just to name a few. He also loved barbershop music, and sang and taught it for fifty years.

The Land of the Sky Barbershop Chorus sang at his memorial. I am certain that he was there in spirit. In fact, I caught a glimpse of him directing behind the first director with his hips moving and his whole body saying, "Let's give it more oomph!"

Now, as I lay reminiscing about him, I, again, heard the words, "Go to your computer, and write about this in your book."

The words seemed to be coming from Skip, and I typed as he spoke.

"The music of the heavenly realms includes thousands and thousands of legions of magnificent angels, along with the beautiful souls and light bodies of the beings on many planets and dimensions. All souls of the heavenly realms like me, who want to concentrate on music of the most high, are called together. When we come together and blend our heavenly voices, we become one in accord. In other words, we can telepathically converse, transpose, compose, and so on.

When we want to be heard all over the heavens and lift up our voices to God, the Maker, and Creator of All, we form our vocal cords into one instrument, and replicate a kind of united vocal cord mechanism. Only this instrument is quite finely tuned, and when we all come together as one voice, we incorporate such melodious sounds of a frequency unlike anything one has ever heard. For remember, these sounds are of perfect pitch, harmony, and melody, and the chords they ring out are the most amazing tones ever heard. It literally fills up the heavens and all creatures great and small can pick up these vibrations. The vibrations give out a healing and soothing energy that resonates within the mind, body and soul of the human species, even though they cannot hear it with their ears. This is why the Master Christ said to 'Be still and listen.'

"I am a singer as well as a player with the heavenly chorus and so happy with my heavenly assignment and home base. It is my joy to have the Earth ring with harmony and vibration to bring about the oneness of souls with this healing. People on Earth only get a glimpse and feeling of this unity, but once humans make their transition, they will experience the reality of the Oneness of All!

"Everyone is equal in status where I am, and no one is judged, but only accepted with wide openness, love, and respect. It is utopia; no worries, heartaches, or illness here.

"I was escorted to this home in the Third Universe by three beautiful angels. Then, when I arrived, there was a host of more angels along with all the souls that were family, friends, and group souls while on the Earth. There were many guides present in this realm similar to the many guides that always accompany us on our Earthly journey.

"I am so happy that you, Ethel, can converse with me as, well as other beings such as those of the Blue Crystal Planet who are extremely advanced beings, and want to help the Earth inhabitants move into their true fourth- and fifth-dimensional selves.

"Here, where I reside, there are so many more choices of work, play, and creation than on Earth, that it can become almost overwhelming. However, it never gets to the point of emotional stress and disease such as there is in the Earth plane. Here, if we feel disconnected, the angels and guides quickly assist to bring us into accord and alignment. It is much easier in this dimension because there is perfection in varying levels, and complete tolerance for each person's path. We are always striving to become the ultimate perfection, or oneness and merge with the God source.

"I chose to reside in the Music of the Spheres dimension, so I can always assist with music everywhere, and even resonate with the Earth plane. I already have the ability to observe, or peek in on my Earthly family and friends, and I will always be close in spirit and heart to my wife, Heidi. It is now time for her to continue on with her spiritual path and she, too, will feel freer and more open with her mind, body, and soul while still on the Earth. Her mission is to assist others, as well as develop spiritually. She will soon find her own purpose and happiness. She, in time, will release and let go of her connection with me, for that is in her divine plan. When at last it is her time to make the transition, she will join me in spirit. Until then, my desire is to guide her to reach her own potential, and to honor her own beautiful soul. It is of great importance for you to include this information in your book."

I nodded in complete agreement, and was most grateful for his visit. With a sweet touch on my face and whispering we would continue to be in contact, Skip swirled out of my channeling focus, and my consciousness returned to my desk.

I quietly reflected how all this amazing information truly quieted any questions I had about Skip's continued journey after his transition, and what a thrilling experience he was having! I was honored to be present with him as he made his transition, and I was able to catch a glimpse of his angels, one at each side, and one behind, ready to take him home. These surreal angels were of enormous girth, and their wings were extraordinary bands of iridescent energy of the most beautiful colors. I was able to tell Skip what I was seeing, and for that moment, it gave him comfort.

As I observed the angels escorting him to his heavenly palace and to the realms far beyond, I knew that he was then healthy in his light body and soul, and was ecstatic with joy and freedom. He impressed upon me an image of happily performing somersaults with a buoyant gaiety in his being, saying, "I am well, I am free, I am home."

Suddenly, with a brilliant flash of vibrant intensity, I felt someone else enter my office. The familiarity of the presence made me laugh in delight, as Darius materialized right in front of me, beaming his loving smile. He surrounded me with dazzling, rainbow colors of light which caused me to tingle from head to toe.

"Beloved one," he said, "I have been overhearing your most interesting conversation with your friend, Skip. I hope you did not mind that I was listening on the ethereal sidelines, but we all are one, and there are no secrets here. He brought so much to the information you have already been given regarding life after transition or "death," and it added to the credibility of all that you have received before. He also gave such a magnificent description of the musical experiences in the heavenly spheres.

"How auspicious then, that I come here to invite you to take yet another journey to the Blue Crystal Planet, one that will further enlighten the reader to the creative forces in action on our beloved sister planet to the Earth. Is your energy such that you can come with me?"

I remained invigorated by the vitality of Skip's force-field which surrounded me during his visit, in fact, I sensed he was perhaps a party to my conversation with Darius now.

"I would be honored to take yet another tour of your planet and do have a great curiosity as to how the music and other creative, artistic forces are expressed," I replied. "My energy, indeed, is fresh and invigorated by both Skip's visit, and now, by your delightful presence, so I would love to go."

With that, Darius took my hand, and as my Earthly body remained typing, he drew my light body up, and out of the physical and in moments we emerged into a spiraling eddy of colors that were not of the Earth, but of one of the most striking frequencies I had not yet experienced on the Blue Crystal Planet. I felt so uplifted by the sensations of beauty that were surrounding me, and could not do anything but gaze endlessly as I was led into more and more up-spiraling of intense color.

Darius whispered, "This is the Creative Zone and these beings work on creating and recreating for not only our planet, but for others as well, in the many universes."

As he spoke, we floated on a stream of teal colors into the actual zone where gorgeous beings were working. These beings were magnificent, like none I had seen thus far. On our Earth they would be called the beautiful people, like the models and actors, but here they were a bit distinguished from the others.

Darius continued, "These beings are never jealous or envious of each other, and they honor each other's beauty. They do look like they are more human, as they have a bit more form to them. Other beings around them have a great respect for them, just as Earthlings would have for certain doctors, scientists, writers, and artists."

As he spoke, I was floating into a chamber that was so vast I could not see doors or enclosures from one room to another. Each room flowed into the other, so it was endless and seamless, although there were distinctions of shape. I could hardly believe my eyes or cosmic eyes as I observed them working as individuals or groups in a harmonious fashion.

There was spectacular music, like none I have heard before, in the background. It was so soothing to my soul, that all my selves came together as one, that is, all of my bodies, physical, ethereal, astral, cosmic, were exactly aligned together perfectly, and I felt like I was whole for the first time in my life. The musical notes brought about balance to all the bodies, so they were joined as one, like a perfectly harmonious chord.

I thought I would first see artisans, but, now I was informed that I was in the Chamber of the Musical Spheres and could observe types of instruments that I had not seen previously. They were not of a material that we know, but of a soft, transparent nature that sort of depicted the mechanics of the insides of our current musical instruments on Earth.

These were of varying colors and strings of thread-like substance, and were played with a very quick manipulation using their minds. It was awesome! They did not need sheets of music like we do, but instead used their creative cosmic minds to know what to play. Each musician knew automatically what he needed to do to make the sounds harmonious, and they did not have to struggle with practicing. They did repetitive pieces, but with different intonations and vibrations, so it was like the same theme, but with differing interpretations.

It was astonishing how each note or sound struck a chord within every cellular structure of my body. In addition, I received sensations of oneness with all, healing on all levels within myself, including memory restoration of places I had been, and insights into a new paradigm that I could take back with me to Earth.

As I was observing all of this and trying to communicate what I experienced into my computer, another part of my mind was simultaneously viewing the other chambers of artistic beings creating a type of art work. It was easy to do this with my cosmic mind, but not with my physical brain, which became quite overwhelmed observing two chambers at once.

Finally, I had to resort to asking Darius and the guides to just give me one experience at a time. They were understanding and cooperative about this, and respected my wishes. There was a great feeling of harmony there, and I felt totally free and was in control of my own free will. I thanked them for that and continued to focus on the Music Chamber.

Darius explained, "The music touches on every chord of the receiver, and is healing, soothing, and cleansing simultaneously. It goes out of our Chamber and infiltrates into the Earth's atmosphere in blocks or pieces, which many of your musicians pick up in their brain senses, and think they have composed it themselves. They think they hear it in their head, and those with a passion for music are able to pick it up and complete the piece and share it with the public when it is completed."

Darius continued, "This music is a universal language and certain chords and sounds heard out in the universes are picked up by other cosmic beings, and they, then, will reply and respond in similar fashion. So, music is truly universal and can be interpreted by the many other beings who hear it. When one hears huge choruses come together, it truly is the music of the spheres. They do not have any discord or loud or erroneous intonations like our metal bands or loud music that would harm one's ears or chakras. They do not have a musical director, but a leader that stands among them that they all turn towards with respect. He automatically starts the sounds, and they chime in, but there is no hesitation, and it's as if they read his mind. All are in accord and begin together."

I observed these beings as they came together in harmony and the many different hues reflecting the different frequencies as they blended together as one. It looked like the colors of our rainbow, however, there was much more presence of colors that were indescribable, but which emanated a type of feeling of the energy. Every now and then I saw a band of a dominant color, like light gold, as a thread being woven into a type of tapestry of the music. It was so unique!

Each of these beings was also a musical instrument unto themselves. They used their bodies as instruments, going far beyond just vocal cords or lungs, but their entire being or life force, was employed to bring forth sound. They did not have to practice such as we would, but had a knowing when to come together in this way. How they did this, I do not know.

Darius saw my amazement, as I tried to comprehend how all this came together.

He said, "On your planet, you communicate with your vocal cords and hear with your ears, along with your five senses. Well, here, you only have to bring people together because each has their own vibration. In other words, if you want a lead or soprano, you only have to ask the soprano vibration to get together with other singing parts such as base, tenor, alto, or baritone. However, there are many more musical sounds that you cannot hear with the natural human abilities that you have. Again, there are millions of sopranos, and those of each singing part all over this universe and the Blue Crystal Planet as well. They volunteer to come together in one accord."

There is so much I had to learn, and they told me that I will learn more as we go along. Darius gently nudged me in the direction of another chamber. He began to describe it to me.

"This is the Chamber of Artists. The artists manipulate their various frequencies in a way so that they can manifest things that you will be able to see with your naked eye, similarly as you do on the Earth plane. You can actually see their cosmic minds work in a most creative manner unknown to mankind. They think out a thought or creative idea that takes a type of form. However, if it is not to their likening, they just erase it with their mind, and start again. It's like writing or drawing on a piece of canvas or paper, then going over it to change it, or completely starting it again on a new piece of paper.

"Now, here's the interesting part. They can create masterpieces of art or sculpture with materials that mankind has never known. However, what is so amazing is that these are not small works of art, but humongous, for the most part, yet, they can transport these items out into the universe to whatever destination they desire. The item actually floats and rides on waves in such quick fashion, that once you see it, then you don't. It is similar in manner to how beings transport themselves around the many universes, in what you call spaceships. Your naked eye sometimes catches a glimpse of them, and then in a twinkling, they are out of sight."

"Simply amazing," I murmured, still trying to grasp the concept.

Darius continued, "These huge masterpieces are done by groups working harmoniously together. Then, there are individual types that work on smaller pieces or projects."

I was able to see one piece of art being developed by a sculptor. It was difficult to distinguish what material he was using, but it resembled a solid piece of hard material, but was so soft and pliable, that I could put my hand through it when I touched it, yet this did not disturb its components. The artist allowed me to see the creation of this with my mind in very slow motion by decreasing the molecular movement of the atoms. Then, it looked like he drew it first in his mind, then moved different materials together and pulled them together in form. So, on my level, it looked like a piece of architectural sculpture, likened to a spiral building. It was magnificent, and quite different in that it could be viewed in a three dimensional form, or like a hologram of the fourth-, fifth-, or sixth-dimension. This really blew my mind. I felt like I was in a foreign country, only in outer space, and nothing looked familiar to me or could be identified or described accurately.

Then Darius and the guides led me to a chamber where lovely softly colored beings were painting or working on a mural. This was a mural of the genealogy and history of the planet Earth with a type of beginning, present, and future. It was unlike anything I had ever seen! The guides told me that our prophets of old were given this information which was considered part of the secrets of the universe. This mural was so vast, that I could not take it all in or see the completion or ending it portrayed. They told me it was because the Earth is not in its completion yet. If they allowed me to know the future, it would be so advanced for my brain and thinking, that I could not comprehend it. They did tell me they will give me future renderings which will be in a second book and not to fear, for there will be interceptors and guidance for the Earth so its destruction will not be permitted.

As I viewed the mural, I was overcome by the depictions which were so unique, and the colors were so vivid that they almost blinded me!

The guide explained, "We are creating this mural to bring in the information and the new text for our future Earth endowment, and the changes that are coming will bring about more peace and understanding. Never lose hope, but have faith and know that the God source has sent legions of angelic beings to assist the Earth as well, and that the beings of the Blue Crystal Planet are only one group of various spirit or ethereal guides which are assisting in bringing in the new paradigm. When you pray to the gods and to the lords and to your spirit guides, it is all the same for it is forwarded instantly to the God source, and all are in accord in their tasks."

Darius was at my side and added to what the guide had just spoken. "We are all instruments of God, and it is important how we use these instruments which should always be for the good of oneself, and the highest good of all others. When the people of the Earth practice and practice whether it be instruments, or our own voices, keep in mind to always think in the light or light waves, for this is as close to perfection as they can come. This is how you, Ethel, are able to channel information. It is much more accessible, and more in tune with the way the heavenly realms and the other many dimensions operate. It is free flowing, and almost without the tedious, strenuous type of thinking. It just comes, and one does not even need words to be able to communicate.

"Teach others how to use this technique, if that's what you want to call, it. Your mathematicians are now able to put this in a formula, or explain in math concepts. Soon, we will be able to give you more details on this when the right time, or conditions are available to you."

I was reflecting on what Darius and the guide had just said when I realized I was fully back in my physical body sitting at my computer. I sensed a permeating, flowery fragrance which reminded me that Darius had just been present.

Much had been experienced and learned, yet I knew there was much more yet to come. I was most excited to relate all I had experienced with Bert, who was also quite close to our friend, Skip, and being musically inclined himself, would love hearing about the vastness of the musical spheres.

ONE LAST THING

Since I have written this book, the Blue Crystal beings have appeared to me numerous times. They appear to be tall, crystalline, humanoid forms, with iridescent hues that emit a type of cosmic, heavenly light and a high frequency of the love vibration. They have pointed heads, and continuously inform me that, although we see them as a type of extraterrestrial, they are truly our galactic sisters and brothers from our sister planet. Among their many duties, they have been called upon and assigned to become the planet Earth's caretakers.

They have appeared to many others on this planet and are working diligently to assist us in our evolving. Their plan is to allow us to tune into them, and to their being, whereby, we would have the ability to raise our frequency from third-dimension to fourth-, fifth-, sixth-, and seventh- and beyond

They stated in numerous ways how we have been stuck in our third-dimensional illusion for eons of time, and their hope is that we can shed and release the illusion, and see who we truly are. When we are in prayer, meditation, and a higher frequency the beings see the more perfected entities that we are, and, so, they continue to help those who want assistance to step out of the illusion and the old ways of thinking into the new way of "knowing." When we can allow ourselves to go into our knowing, we will then have the ability to see them clearly, recognize their frequency, and converse. It is their hope that one day soon we can coexist side by side with them, as well as beings from other planets. Humans will recognize that we all come from the God source and we are all one.

In working with them, we will learn more about what we have forgotten over eons of times, and that our memory banks will open up to empower us to know the ancient truths, and the celestial teachings that we have forgotten for ever so long. When we reach that state towards our ascension, we will begin to use the God-given abilities that were given when we first incarnated into this amazing planet, Earth. We will have the ability to speak the universal language by a type of telepathy. We will be able to heal ourselves and others in natural ways, as well. We will love one another equally and unconditionally, and in a non-judgmental manner. We will create a new world that is loving, peaceful, and global among all peoples, all cultures and all species. We will have the ability to manifest those things that we desire for our highest good. We will be ever so grateful to be here on this sweet planet that nourishes us and assists us in the greater knowledge of all things. We will appreciate our travels to the Blue Crystal Planet, as well as visitations to other planets, stars, galaxies and the universe.

More detailed information will be given in future writings so that we can better understand our relationship with our brothers and sisters beyond the Earth . . . and so it is, and so mote it be . . . this has been a blessed and enlightening gift to the author of these writings, and much more will come at a later time.

SPECIAL THANKS

Special thanks to Linda Aurora Fox, for the many long hours of work on editing and placing the book in "Story form." It is with great honor and appreciation that I thank her for all her efforts.

ABOUT THE AUTHOR

Ethel E. Crites, (Anastasia), B.A., Educational Psychology, M. ed. Guidance/Counseling, world-renowned clairvoyant, leads the reader on a spiritually awakening journey to our sister planet, called the Blue Crystal Planet, located in the Third Galaxy. Intuitively, her explorations reveal an amazing world of loving, wise, and compassionate beings who are assisting humanity in awakening to the potential of who they truly are. As she journeys on the various tours of the planet, she brings back tools that further equip humans to join in the inevitable, higher dimensional paradigm that is awaiting them as the Earth evolves into the fifth-dimension. Ethel channeled this material using her ability to think "in the light" and "be in the light with All that Is."

Featured on television and radio shows throughout the United States, Ethel is an outstanding and amazing intuitive. She has been gifted with cosmic knowledge about the universes, planets and galaxies. Ethel is widely known as a teacher, counselor, and healer, and is an Ordained Minister with the Brigade of Light. She has done extensive research with the Paranormal Research Project at Poseida Institute, Virginia Beach, Virginia and has spent over twenty years as a family and individual counselor, social worker and school teacher. She has done invaluable intuitive criminal investigations for missing persons and pets with various government agencies. She is currently available for lectures and private spiritual consultations.

You may contact her at angelguide.ethel@yahoo.com.

CPSIA information can be obtained
at www.ICGtesting.com
Printed in the USA
FFOW05n1153140216